Accounting for AQA
A-level Part 1

Question Bank

David Cox

© David Cox, 2021.

All rights reserved. No part of this publication may be reproduced, stored in a retrieval system, or transmitted in any form or by any means, electronic, mechanical, photo-copying, recording or otherwise, without the prior consent of the copyright owners, or in accordance with the provisions of the Copyright, Designs and Patents Act 1988, or under the terms of any licence permitting limited copying issued by The Copyright Licensing Agency, Saffron House, 6-10 Kirby Street, London EC1N 8TS.

Published by Osborne Books Limited
Tel 01905 748071
Email books@osbornebooks.co.uk
Website www.osbornebooks.co.uk

British Library Cataloguing in Publication Data
A catalogue record for this book is available from the British Library

ISBN 978-1-911198-90-1

Contents

		Questions	Answers
	Introduction to Financial Accounting		
1-6	Double-entry procedures; Business documents	2	128
7	The cash book	14	137
8	Bank reconciliation statements	19	140
9	Introduction to financial statements	26	143
10	The general journal and correction of errors	33	146
11	Control accounts	37	148
12	Adjustments to financial statements	44	151
	Financial Accounting		
13	Business organisations and financing	58	160
14	Accounting concepts and inventory valuation	63	163
15	Further aspects of financial statements	67	165
16	Preparing sole trader financial statements	76	170
17	Financial statements of limited companies	85	176
18	Financial ratios	93	180
	Management Accounting		
19	Budgeting and budgetary control	102	184
20	Marginal costing and break-even	110	189
21	Decision-making situations	116	192

Introduction

Accounting for AQA A-level Part 1 Question Bank has been written to provide supplementary examination practice material for students of AQA's A-level in Accounting.

The book is divided into two separate sections:

1 **Questions** appropriate for the AQA examinations, with gaps where students can write in the answers.

2 **Answers** to each of the questions, set out in the fully worked layout that should be used.

The book is also arranged in the chapter order of the main text book, **Accounting for AQA A-level Part 1** (see the Contents on the previous page). There are questions and answers for each of the chapters, with the exception of Chapters 1 to 6, where the questions have been amalgamated into one longer section for ease of use.

David Cox

Use of Accounting Terminology

The AQA examinations in Accounting make full use of international terminology as set out in International Financial Reporting Standards (IFRSs). The following shows the international terminology, together with the terminology used previously.

International Terminology	Terminology used previously
Financial statements	
Cash and cash equivalents (limited companies)	Cash in hand, cash at bank/bank overdraft
Financial statements	Final accounts and balance sheets
Income statement	Trading and profit and loss account
Inventory	Stock
Irrecoverable debt	Bad debt
Loss for year	Net loss
Non-current assets	Fixed assets
Non-current liabilities	Long-term liabilities
Other payables	Expenses due; income received in advance
Other receivables	Expenses prepaid; income due
Profit for year	Net profit
Revenue (within an income statement)	Sales
Statement of financial position	Balance sheet
Trade payables	Trade creditors (creditors)
Trade receivables	Trade debtors (debtors)
Accounting ratios	
Expenses in relation to revenue %	Expenses in relation to sales %
Profit to revenue %	Net profit to sales %
Rate of inventory turnover	Rate of stock turnover
Trade payable days	Creditor payment period
Trade receivable days	Debtor collection period

Practice questions

Introduction to Financial Accounting   page 2

Financial Accounting   page 58

Management Accounting   page 102

INTRODUCTION TO FINANCIAL ACCOUNTING
QUESTIONS

CHAPTERS 1-6: DOUBLE-ENTRY PROCEDURES; BUSINESS DOCUMENTS

The questions in this section deal with the basics of accounting. They cover topics such as:

- keeping accounting records
- stakeholders in a business
- business documents
- double-entry bookkeeping
- books of prime entry
- the trial balance

The reason for grouping them together is that often at this early stage of accounting, examination questions typically cover more than one topic. For later chapters, individual questions have been identified which relate to a particular chapter.

1. Al Porter has started a new business which is financed by £20,000 from his personal savings and a bank loan of £10,000.

    (a) Explain **two** reasons why Al should keep accounting records.

    Reason 1

    ....

    ....

    ....

    ....

    ....

Reason 2

....

....

....

....

....

(b) Identify **three** external stakeholders in Al's business. State the interest they will have in the accounting records.

Stakeholder 1

....

....

....

....

Stakeholder 2

....

....

....

....

Stakeholder 3

....

....

....

....

2. Alcaria is a wholesale business. At 1 May 20-4, Sam Brass owed Alcaria £745. During May 20-4, the following transactions took place:

   7 May   Alcaria sold goods to Sam Brass for £275

   16 May   Sam Brass returned goods valued at £84 to Alcaria

   24 May   Sam Brass sent a cheque, after deducting a cash discount of £18, to Alcaria to clear the balance owing at 1 May

   (a) Identify the source document used by Alcaria to record each of the above transactions.

Transaction	Source document
Alcaria sold goods to Sam Brass for £275	
Sam Brass returned goods valued at £84 to Alcaria	
Sam Brass sent a cheque, after deducting a cash discount of £18, to Alcaria to clear the balance owing at 1 May	

   (b) Complete the account of Sam Brass in the books of Alcaria for the month of May 20-4.

Dr			Sam Brass			Cr
Date	Details	£	Date	Details		£

3. Hayley Ortez runs a clothes shop. Two of her recent business transactions are:

Item 1: The payment of wages by cheque

Item 2: The return of goods to a supplier. The goods had previously been purchased on credit

(a) Complete the following table by entering the appropriate details in the spaces provided.

Item	Source document	Account to be debited	Account to be credited
1			
2			

The following transactions took place between Hayley Ortez and Fashion Frocks, a credit supplier, during June 20-1.

1 June	Balance brought forward £1,275	
8 June	Goods bought on credit by Hayley Ortez, £950	
12 June	Hayley Ortez makes a bank transfer to Fashion Frocks for £1,205; cash discount received £70	
18 June	Hayley Ortez returns goods to Fashion Frocks, £150	
23 June	Goods bought on credit by Hayley Ortez, £650	

(b) Complete the purchases ledger account of Fashion Frocks in the books of Hayley Ortez. Balance the account at 30 June 20-1.

Dr   Fashion Frocks   Cr

Date	Details	£	Date	Details	£

4. Michel Cavares owns a business which sells shoes. The following transactions took place in March 20-9:

(a) Identify the source document for each of the following transactions.

Transaction	Source document
Shoes from a manufacturer purchased on credit	
Michel returned shoes to a manufacturer which had previously been purchased on credit	
Cash and cheques deposited by Michel into the business bank account	
Michel paid a supplier by cheque	
Michel sold 50 pairs of trainers to a sports centre. Payment will be made next month	

(b) Complete the following table by entering the appropriate details in the spaces provided. (Note that Michel's accounting system does not use control accounts.)

Transaction	Account to be debited	Account to be credited
A new shop till purchased from AJ Supplies on credit for £1,000		
£5,000 paid into the business bank account from Michel's savings		
Paid £1,200 to Shoe Traders, a supplier, in settlement of the account balance		
Paid shop rent of £750 by bank transfer		

5. Assess the usefulness of the trial balance as a means of checking the accuracy of the ledgers.

6. A business has bought goods for resale on credit from a supplier.

   How should the purchase of the goods be recorded in the accounting system of the business?

	Book of prime entry	Debit	Credit
A	Purchases journal	Purchases	Supplier
B	Purchases returns journal	Supplier	Purchases returns
C	Purchases journal	Purchases	Bank
D	Purchases journal	Supplier	Purchases

7. A business has sold goods in which it trades on credit to a customer. The goods are faulty and are returned by the customer.

   How should the return of the goods be recorded in the accounting system of the business?

	Book of prime entry	Debit	Credit
A	Sales returns journal	Customer	Sales returns
B	Sales journal	Customer	Sales returns
C	Sales returns journal	Sales returns	Customer
D	Sales journal	Customer	Sales

8. A business has received a credit note.

   What entries should be made in the business's ledger accounts?

	Account debited	Account credited
A	Purchases returns	Trade payable
B	Trade payable	Sales returns
C	Sales returns	Trade receivable
D	Trade payable	Purchases returns

9. The following is an extract from the cash book of Mark Kirwan for April 20-7.

Required:

(a) Balance the following bank account at 30 April 20-7, showing the balance brought down on 1 May 20-7, and transfer cash discounts to the appropriate accounts.

Dr   **Bank Account**   Cr

Date 20-7	Details	Discount £	Bank £	Date 20-7	Details	Discount £	Bank £
26 Apr	Balance b/d		246	27 Apr	J Khan		332
27 Apr	A Monro		116	30 Apr	Raven Ltd	16	746
28 Apr	A Syed	10	425				

GENERAL LEDGER

Dr   **Discount Allowed**   Cr

Date 20-7	Details	£	Date 20-7	Details	£

Dr   **Discount Received**   Cr

Date 20-7	Details	£	Date 20-7	Details	£

The following are extracts from the books of prime entry of Mark Kirwan for April 20-7.

Sales Journal

Date	Details	Amount £
6 Apr	A Monro	316
8 Apr	A Syed	435

Purchases Journal

Date	Details	Amount £
11 Apr	J Khan	454
13 Apr	Raven Ltd	762

Required:

(b) Record the entries from the sales journal and the purchases journal, and from the bank account, into the accounts below. Balance the accounts at 30 April 20-7, showing the balance brought down on 1 May 20-7 where appropriate.

SALES LEDGER

Dr — A Monro — Cr

Date 20-7	Details	£	Date 20-7	Details	£

Dr — A Syed — Cr

Date 20-7	Details	£	Date 20-7	Details	£

PURCHASES LEDGER

Dr   J Khan   Cr

Date 20-7	Details	£	Date 20-7	Details	£
			1 Apr	Balance b/d	332

Dr   Raven Ltd   Cr

Date 20-7	Details	£	Date 20-7	Details	£

10. Eve Birch owns a retail business. Her bookkeeper has been preparing the business's accounting records for June 20-4, but the following has not yet been recorded:

Date 20-4	Source document	Details
23 June	Purchases invoice	A Sanders for goods with a list price of £2,000 less a trade discount of 15%.
25 June	Bank statement	Settled the amount due to T Smithers on 1 June by bank transfer, less a 5% cash discount.
26 June	Credit note	Received from A Sanders as one-quarter of the goods bought on 23 June were not as ordered.
27 June	Cheque counterfoil	Cheque to P Yarnton in settlement of the amount currently due, less a 2% cash discount.
29 June	Purchases invoice	P Yarnton for goods with a list price of £1,200 less a trade discount of 12%.

(a) Record the transactions above in the business's books of prime entry shown below.

BOOKS OF PRIME ENTRY

PURCHASES JOURNAL		
20-4		£

PURCHASES RETURNS JOURNAL		
20-4		£

BANK ACCOUNT					
20-4		£	20-4		£
1 Jun	Balance b/d	1,027			

(b) Record the transactions above in the business's purchases (payables) ledger shown below.

PURCHASES (PAYABLES) LEDGER

A SANDERS ACCOUNT					
20-4		£	20-4		£

T SMITHERS ACCOUNT					
20-4		£	20-4		£
			1 Jun	Balance b/d	440

P YARNTON ACCOUNT					
20-4		£	20-4		£
10 Jun	Purchases returns journal	130	1 Jun	Balance b/d	280

(c) Record the relevant transactions above in the business's discount received account shown below.

DISCOUNT RECEIVED ACCOUNT					
20-4		£	20-4		£

11. (a) Explain, using examples, the work carried out by a bookkeeper within the financial accounting system.

....

....

....

(b) Explain, using examples, how the work carried out by an accountant differs from that of a bookkeeper.

....

....

....

CHAPTER 7: THE CASH BOOK

1. Al Porter has started a new business and has opened a business bank account.
   Explain the meaning of each of the following terms, together with an example of their use, in relation to Al's bank account.

   (i) Direct debit

   (ii) Standing order

2. The balances in Sally Henshaw's three column cash book at 3 August 20-7 were as follows:

	£
Cash	286
Bank overdraft	3,472

The following transactions took place:

3 Aug	Paid rent by cheque £760
4 Aug	Cash sales £334
5 Aug	Banked £500 cash from the till
5 Aug	Received a bank transfer of £1,475 from Murphy Ltd in full settlement of a debt of £1,490
8 Aug	Paid rates by direct debit £223
8 Aug	Paid JJ Supplies by bank transfer £490 after deducting 2% cash discount
10 Aug	Withdrew £400 cash from the bank for business use
10 Aug	Paid wages £480 in cash

Required:

Enter the above transactions in the cash book on the next page and balance the cash book at 10 August 20-7.

Cash Book

Dr										Cr
Date 20-7	Details	Discount £	Cash £	Bank £	Date 20-7	Details	Discount £	Cash £	Bank £

3. Emma Maxwell uses a three-column cash book as part of her double-entry bookkeeping system. The following details relate to March 20-3.

March			£
1		Balance in cash account	200
		Overdrawn bank balance	1,898
2		Bank transfer made to Lindum Supplies in settlement of an invoice for £260	254
6		Cheque from Court Ltd paid into bank	1,236
11		Paid rent by cheque	550
13		Bank transfer received from H Sweeney. Discount of £10 had been taken by the customer	896
14		Cash sales	639
27		Paid wages of part-time employee in cash	155
28		Cash sales	786

A bank statement received on 28 March revealed the following additional items.

20		Standing order to Wyvern Council	195
21		Interest charged by bank	45
24		Bank transfer received from Mills and Co Ltd	477

On 31 March all cash, except a float of £200, was paid into the bank.

Required:

(a) Prepare the cash book, shown on the next page, for the month of March 20-3 from the information provided above.

(b) Balance the cash book at the end of the month and bring down the balances at 1 April 20-3.

(c) Record the discounts in the general ledger accounts shown below the cash book.

Dr					Emma Maxwell Cash Book					Cr
Date 20-3	Details	Discount £	Cash £	Bank £	Date 20-3	Details	Discount £	Cash £	Bank £

Dr			Discount Allowed Account			Cr
Date 20-3	Details	£	Date 20-3	Details	£

Dr			Discount Received Account			Cr
Date 20-3	Details	£	Date 20-3	Details	£

CHAPTER 8: BANK RECONCILIATION STATEMENTS

1. Show whether the following statements are true or false.

Statement		True	False
(a)	Some differences between the bank statement and the cash book are described as timing differences – these are not corrected in the cash book		
(b)	A trade receivable's cheque has been dishonoured and returned by the bank – the amount of the dishonoured cheque must be recorded in cash book on the debit side		
(c)	In a bank reconciliation statement which starts with the cash book balance, unpresented cheques are added		
(d)	The opening cash book balance at bank will always be the same as the opening bank statement balance		

2. Complete the following text by choosing the correct words from the boxes below and entering them in the boxes in the text.

cash book	bank statement	ledger	error
discrepancy	fraud	regular	daily
timing	date	independent	similarity

It is important to reconcile the cash book to the _____ on a _____ basis.

The bank statement provides an _____ accounting record and helps to prevent _____ .

It also highlights any _____ differences and explains why there is a _____ between the bank statement balance and the _____ balance.

3. Jayne Carter's cash book showed a debit balance of £743. This did not agree with the closing balance on her bank statement, dated 27 April 20-1.

The following entries appear on the bank statement but have not been entered in the cash book.

(1) Bank charges of £25

(2) A direct debit payment of £220 to Wyvern Council

(3) A bank transfer of £455 from Alportal Ltd

(4) A cheque received from L Johnson, dishonoured by the customer's bank. The cheque for £105 had been debited in Jayne Carter's cash book on 20 April 20-1.

Jayne also discovered that a direct debit for £45 paid to A Alta on 25 April 20-1 appeared on the bank statement correctly, but had been entered in the cash book as £54.

The following entries appear in the cash book but do not yet appear on the bank statement.

(1) A cheque for £126 paid to S Brass on 25 April 20-1

(2) Takings of £275 banked on 27 April 20-1

Required:

(a) Make the necessary entries in the cash book of Jayne Carter and bring down the balance at 27 April 20-1. Dates are not required.

Dr   Cash Book (bank columns)   Cr

Details	£	Details	£
Balance b/d	743		

(b) Prepare a bank reconciliation statement at 27 April 20-1.

Bank Reconciliation Statement at 27 April 20-1

....

....

....

....

....

....

....

....

....

....

....

(c) Explain **three** reasons why it is important for Jayne Carter to reconcile her cash book and bank statement balances.

1 ....

....

....

2 ....

....

....

3 ....

....

....

4. The cash book of Susana Villona's business shows a bank overdraft of £2,408 at 30 September 20-4. The balance shown on the bank statement at that date does not agree with the balance shown in the cash book.

The following points are discovered.

(1) A direct debit payment of £485 on 28 September 20-4 to A-Z Finance Ltd has not yet been entered in the cash book.

(2) A cheque payment of £750 on 29 September 20-4 for rent paid has been entered in the cash book but has not yet been presented to the bank.

(3) On 30 September 20-4, the bank debited the account with interest and charges of £124. This amount has not been entered in the cash book.

(4) A cheque received from a customer for £368 on 29 September 20-4 has been paid into the bank and entered in the cash book. The transaction is not shown on the bank statement.

(5) A bank transfer made to a supplier on 23 September 20-4 appears on the bank statement as £465 but has been incorrectly entered in the cash book as £645.

Required:

(a) Make the necessary entries in the cash book of Susana Villona and show the updated balance at 30 September 20-4. Dates are not required.

Dr		Cash Book (bank columns)		Cr
Details	£	**Details**		£
		Balance b/d		2,408

(b) Prepare a bank reconciliation statement for Susana Villona that clearly shows the balance on the bank statement at 30 September 20-4.

(c) Explain why Susana Villona's bank may require a copy of her year-end financial statements.

5. On 30 June Durning Trading received a bank statement as at 27 June 20-8:

BANK STATEMENT

20-8		Paid out £	Paid in £	Balance £
1 Jun	Balance brought forward			768 C
2 Jun	Cheque 364125	427		341 C
3 Jun	Bacs credit: Asif Ltd		1,122	1,463 C
18 Jun	Cheque 364127	4,200		2,737 D
20 Jun	Direct debit: JC Property Co	850		3,587 D
23 Jun	Bacs credit: Sand & Stone		2,486	1,101 D
26 Jun	Bacs credit: Surfrider Ltd		4,110	3,009 C
27 Jun	Direct debit: Vord Finance	275		2,734 C
27 Jun	Cheque 364128	1,062		1,672 C

D = Debit   C = Credit

The cash book of Durning Trading as at 27 June 20-8 is shown below:

CASH BOOK

Date	Details	Bank	Date	Cheque no	Details	Bank
20-8		£	20-8			£
1 Jun	Balance b/d	1,890	1 Jun	364125	Penryn Ltd	427
20 Jun	Chiverton Ltd	1,200	3 Jun	364126	Fal Boats	760
24 Jun	Perran Ltd	4,750	10 Jun	364127	S Mawes	4,200
24 Jun	P Porth	8,950	20 Jun	364128	Castle Supplies	1,062

You are to:

(a) Check the items on the bank statement against the items in the cash book.

(b) Update the cash book as needed.

(c) Total the cash book and clearly show the balance carried down at 27 June and brought down at 28 June 20-8.

(d) Prepare a bank reconciliation statement as at 27 June 20-8.

Durning Trading
Bank Reconciliation Statement as at 27 June 20-8

	£	£

CHAPTER 9: INTRODUCTION TO FINANCIAL STATEMENTS

1. The following trial balance has been extracted by the bookkeeper of Samantha Giardino at 31 December 20-7:

	Dr £	Cr £
Trade receivables	24,365	
Trade payables		19,871
Bank overdraft		2,454
Capital at 1 January 20-7		51,283
Revenue (Sales)		188,622
Purchases	110,233	
Inventory at 1 January 20-7	21,945	
Salaries	37,390	
Heating and lighting	4,276	
Rent and business rates	6,849	
Vehicles	20,450	
Office equipment	10,960	
Sundry expenses	1,283	
Vehicle expenses	3,562	
Drawings	20,917	
	262,230	262,230

Inventory at 31 December 20-7 is valued at £18,762.

You are to prepare the income statement of Samantha Giardino for the year ended 31 December 20-7, together with her statement of financial position at that date.

Samantha Giardino
Income Statement
for the year ended 31 December 20-7

£ £

Statement of Financial Position as at 31 December 20-7

£   £   £

2. Alan Castle has part-completed his income statement for the year ended 30 June 20-3.

From the following information:

(a) Complete the income statement for the year ended 30 June 20-3, commencing with gross profit.

	£
Gross profit	55,430
Salaries and wages	47,390
Discount received	210
Office expenses	2,750
Vehicle expenses	6,840
Bank charges	570
Drawings	8,460
Capital	42,170

Alan Castle
Income Statement
for the year ended 30 June 20-3

(b) Prepare Alan Castle's capital account as at 30 June 20-3.

Dr			Capital Account		Cr
Date 20-3	Details	£	Date 20-3	Details	£

3. The following information was provided by a sole trader for the year ended 30 June 20-9.

	£
Capital 1 July 20-8	65,000
Capital 30 June 20-9	69,000
Drawings	18,000

What was the business's profit or loss for the year ended 30 June 20-9?

A	loss £4,000	
B	loss £22,000	
C	profit £4,000	
D	profit £22,000	

4. From the following figures complete the statement of financial position for PQ Trading as at 30 September 20-2. Clearly show the non-current and current assets, non-current and current liabilities, and the proprietor's capital.

	£
Profit for the year	24,550
Inventory at 30 September 20-2	16,345
Trade receivables	24,540
Trade payables	21,364
Property	175,000
Office equipment	16,450
Bank overdraft	5,145
Cash	496
Drawings	21,000
Mortgage on business premises	100,000

PQ Trading
Statement of Financial Position as at 30 September 20-2

CHAPTER 10: THE GENERAL JOURNAL AND CORRECTION OF ERRORS

1. The following errors have been made in the accounting records of Beacon Traders. Tick to show which of the errors below are, or are not, disclosed by the trial balance.

Error in the general ledger	Error disclosed by the trial balance	Error not disclosed by the trial balance
A bank payment for telephone expenses has been recorded on the debit side of both the cash book and telephone expenses account		
A payment recorded in bank account for vehicle repairs has been entered in vehicles account		
A sales invoice has been omitted from all accounting records		
The balance of purchases returns account has been calculated incorrectly		
A bank payment of £85 for stationery has been recorded as £58 in both accounts		

2. An amount has been entered into the accounting system as £65 instead of £56. The error is called:

A	Compensating error	
B	Error of commission	
C	Error of principle	
D	Error of original entry	

3. A business bought furniture for use in the office on credit from a supplier. The furniture was delivered scratched and is returned to the supplier.
How should the return of the furniture be recorded in the accounting system of the business?

		Debit	Credit	
A	Purchases returns journal	Purchases returns	Supplier	
B	Purchases returns journal	Supplier	Purchases returns	
C	General journal	Furniture	Supplier	
D	General journal	Supplier	Furniture	

4. The bookkeeper of Alcaria has extracted a trial balance at 31 May 20-3. The totals do not agree and the following errors have been discovered.

(1) The credit balance on the purchases returns account has been brought down as £345. It should be £354.

(2) The purchases account has been undercast by £100.

(3) Discount received of £35 has been entered to the debit of the discount received account.

Make any necessary entries in the suspense account to correct these errors. Clearly show the opening balance on the suspense account and balance the account.

Dr		Suspense Account		Cr
Details	£	**Details**		£

Chapter 10

5. Emma Korecki prepared a trial balance at 30 June 20-7. The trial balance totals are shown below.

　　　Debit　　£364,859　　　　　Credit　　£363,701

She entered the difference in a suspense account and then discovered the following errors.

(1) The discount allowed account has been overcast by £100.

(2) A bank payment of £68 for vehicle expenses has been recorded as £86 in the vehicle expenses account.

(3) Discount received of £40 has been correctly entered in the cash book but has not been posted to the general ledger.

(4) A bank payment of £175 for office stationery has been debited to office equipment account.

(5) A cheque for £500 for rent received has been posted to the debit of rent paid account.

Required:

(a) Enter the difference in the trial balance totals in the suspense account below. Make any necessary entries in the suspense account to correct the errors.

Dr Details	£	Suspense Account Details	Cr £
Discount allowed	100	Balance (difference)	1,158
Vehicle expenses	18		
Discount received	40		
Rent paid	500		
Rent received	500		
	1,158		1,158

(b) Complete the following table to identify the **amount**, if any, by which the profit (net profit) for the year of Emma Korecki would be affected by the **correction** of the errors.

Error	Increase profit £	Reduce profit £	No effect on profit (✓)
(1)			
(2)			
(3)			
(4)			
(5)			

CHAPTER 11: CONTROL ACCOUNTS

1. You have the following information:
- opening customer balances at start of month £18,600
- credit sales for month £9,100
- sales returns for month £800
- payment from customers for month £7,800

What is the figure for closing customer balances at the end of the month?

A	£2,500	
B	£19,100	
C	£19,900	
D	£20,700	

2. You work as an accounts assistant for Durning Traders. Today you are working on the purchases ledger control account and purchases ledger.

A summary of transactions with credit suppliers during May 20-3 is shown below.

	£
Goods purchased on credit	21,587
Payments made to credit suppliers	13,750
Discount received	500
Goods returned to credit suppliers	250

The balance of suppliers at 1 May 20-3 was £50,300.

Required:
Prepare the purchases ledger control account for the month of May 20-3 from the above details. Show clearly the balance carried down at 31 May 20-3.

Purchases Ledger Control Account

Date 20-3	Details	Amount £	Date 20-3	Details	Amount £

3. The following information has been extracted from the books of Chris Santo for the month of April 20-1.

	£
Purchases ledger balances at 1 April 20-1	33,154
Purchases	42,805
Cash purchases	3,241
Payments to trade payables	37,396
Receipts from trade receivables	46,083
Sales returns	1,260
Purchases returns	1,532
Discount allowed	893
Discount received	741
Debit balance on sales ledger set off contra purchases ledger	585
Cheque paid to a trade payable cancelled on 30 April 20-1	842

Required:

(a) Prepare a purchases ledger control account for the month of April 20-1.

Dr			Purchases Ledger Control Account			Cr
Date 20-1	Details	£	Date 20-1	Details		£

(b) Explain how the purchases ledger control account can be used to verify the balances in the purchases ledger.

....

....

....

....

....

....

....

....

....

(c) Explain **one** limitation of the purchases ledger control account and give **one** example.

....

....

....

....

....

....

....

....

....

4. The following information has been extracted from the books of Jenny Tavira for the month of June 20-1.

	£
Sales ledger debit balances at 1 June 20-1	45,027
Sales	61,322
Sales returns	1,475
Bank receipts from trade receivables	55,396
Cash sales	12,784
Discount allowed	1,027
Discount received	648
Debit balance in a sales ledger account set off contra a credit balance in a purchases ledger account	824
Trade receivable's cheque dishonoured	345

Required:

(a) Prepare a sales ledger control account for June 20-1.

Dr			Sales Ledger Control Account			Cr
Date 20-1	**Details**	**£**		**Date 20-1**	**Details**	**£**

(b) Explain how the balance on Jenny Tavira's sales ledger control account verifies the accuracy of her sales ledger.

....
....
....
....
....
....
....

(c) Explain **two** types of error that would **not** be identified by preparing a sales ledger control account.

Error 1 ....
....
....
....
....

Error 2 ....
....
....
....
....

5. Tony Salter owns a business which manufactures shoes. He operates a manual accounting system. The sales ledger control account for the month ended 31 August 20-2 does not agree with the total of the debit balances extracted from the sales ledger.

The following errors have been discovered.

(1) The balance brought down in the sales ledger control account should have been £18,780.

(2) Discount allowed of £125 had been completely omitted from the books of account.

(3) An irrecoverable debt of £220 had been written off, but had not been entered in the sales ledger control account.

(4) The sales journal had been undercast by £1,000.

(5) A debit balance of £175 in the sales ledger had been entered as a contra item in the purchases ledger control account. No entry had been made in the sales ledger control account.

(6) A cheque from a customer for £395 had been dishonoured. This had not been entered in the sales ledger control account.

Required:

(a) Correct the sales ledger control account and balance the account.

Dr			Sales Ledger Control Account			Cr
Date 20-2	Details	£	Date 20-2	Details		£
31 Aug	Balance b/d	18,870				

(b) State **three** benefits of preparing a sales ledger control account.

CHAPTER 12: ADJUSTMENTS TO FINANCIAL STATEMENTS

1. Explain the meaning of the following terms.

    (a) Accrued expenses

    ....

    ....

    ....

    ....

    ....

    ....

    (b) Prepaid expenses

    ....

    ....

    ....

    ....

    ....

    ....

2. The following information is available about rent paid for the year ended 30 June 20-7:

	£
Credit balance brought forward on 1 July 20-6	475
Payments during year ended 30 June 20-7	6,380
Debit balance brought down on 1 July 20-7	650

    How much should be shown as the expense for rent in the income statement for the year ended 30 June 20-7?

A	£5,255	
B	£6,380	
C	£6,205	
D	£7,505	

3. Shelley Smith sells carpets. The following balances have been extracted from the books of account at 31 December 20-3.

	£
Balance at bank	3,130
Capital at 1 January 20-3	22,500
Carriage inwards	1,340
Discount allowed	460
Discount received	970
Drawings	10,030
General expenses	16,450
Inventory at 1 January 20-3	27,170
Purchases	85,210
Rent and business rates	10,160
Sales returns	490
Purchases returns	1,520
Revenue (Sales)	124,380
Shop fitting – at cost	8,300
– provision for depreciation at 1 January 20-3	4,500
Telephone expenses	1,260
Trade payables	10,130

Additional information

(1) Inventory at 31 December 20-3 is valued at £29,210.

(2) The shop fittings are depreciated using the straight-line method over five years. The estimated disposal value of the shop fittings at the end of the fifth year is £800.

(3) Rent unpaid at 31 December 20-3 amounted to £250.

(4) Annual business rates are £1,320. At 31 December 20-3, three months have been paid in advance.

Required:

Prepare the income statement for Shelley Smith for the year ended 31 December 20-3.

Shelley Smith
Income Statement for the year ended 31 December 20-3

£ £

4. Richard Farley sells sports equipment. The following balances have been extracted from his books of account at 31 March 20-3.

	£
Bank loan (repayable September 20-8)	7,600
Bank overdraft	2,580
Capital account at 1 April 20-2	29,250
Carriage inwards	850
Discount allowed	180
Discount received	790
Drawings	15,040
General expenses	11,470
Heating and lighting	2,720
Inventory at 1 April 20-2	24,830
Purchases	76,250
Rent and business rates	18,390
Sales returns	430
Revenue (Sales)	154,360
Shop fittings – at cost	15,200
– provision for depreciation at 1 April 20-2	5,360
Trade payables	6,220
Trade receivables	3,540
Wages and salaries	37,260

Additional information

(1) Inventory at 31 March 20-3 is valued at £26,450.

(2) Annual rent of £10,360 has been paid for the year ending 30 September 20-3.

(3) The shop fittings are to be depreciated using the straight-line method over five years. The estimated disposal value of the shop fittings at the end of the fifth year is £1,800.

(4) On 31 March 20-3 Richard Farley transferred £2,500 from his personal savings into the business bank account. This transaction has not yet been accounted for.

(5) An irrecoverable debt of £240 was to be written off at 31 March 20-3.

(6) Wages and salaries of £830 for the week ended 31 March 20-3 have not yet been paid.

Required:

(a) Prepare the income statement for Richard Farley for the year ended 31 March 20-3.

Richard Farley
Income Statement for the year ended 31 March 20-3

	£	£

(b) Prepare the statement of financial position for Richard Farley at 31 March 20-3.

Richard Farley: Statement of Financial Position at 31 March 20-3

£ £

5. Susie Leah has prepared the following statement of financial position for her business. It contains errors and the totals do not agree.

Susie Leah
Statement of Financial Position as at 31 December 20-6

	£000	£000
Non-current Assets		
Property at cost	220	
Office equipment at cost	60	
		280
Current Assets		
Inventory	18	
Drawings	20	
Bank overdraft	6	
Profit for the year	22	
	66	
Less Current Liabilities		
Trade payables	18	
Trade receivables	15	
Other receivables (prepaid expenses)	3	
Office equipment – provision for depreciation	35	
Other payables (accrued expenses)	2	
	73	
Net Current Liabilities		(7)
Net Assets		273
Capital		
Balance at 1 January 20-6		103
Mortgage on premises (repayable 20-9)		150
		253

Additional information not yet recorded in the books of account

(1) £3,000 rent owed by Susie.

(2) A trade receivable paid £2,000 on 31 December 20-6.

(3) An irrecoverable debt of £1,000 is to be written off at 31 December 20-6.

Required:

Prepare the corrected statement of financial position of Susie Leah taking account of the additional information.

Susie Leah: Statement of Financial Position as at 31 December 20-6

	£000	£000

6. Lydia Duarte owns a business selling building materials. She has prepared the following draft income statement for the year ended 30 September 20-5.

	£
Revenue (Sales)	304,400
Cost of sales	(179,600)
Gross profit for the year	124,800
Expenses	(99,800)
Profit for the year	25,000

After completion of the draft income statement, the following balances remain in the books of account.

	£
Accrued expenses	590
Bank overdraft	2,150
Capital at 1 October 20-4	42,440
Drawings	13,760
Inventory at 30 September 20-5	36,430
Loan (repayable 31 December 20-5)	12,000
Prepaid expenses	730
Trade payables	16,150
Trade receivables	24,310
Vehicles – cost at 1 October 20-4	38,500
– provision for depreciation at 1 October 20-4	15,400

Lydia has been told that the following items have not yet been accounted for.

(1) Wages owing at 30 September 20-5 amounted to £1,480.

(2) Rent paid in advance at 30 September 20-5 amounted to £1,100.

(3) Depreciation is to be provided on vehicles at 20% per annum using the straight-line method.

(4) The value of inventory at 30 September 20-5 has been understated by £2,000.

(5) A loan repayment of £1,000 appeared on the bank statement on 30 September 20-5, but has not been recorded in the accounting records.

(6) A bank transfer for £800 received from a trade receivable on 30 September 20-5 has not been recorded in the accounting records.

(7) A trade receivable's balance of £250 is to be written off as irrecoverable.

Required:

(a) Calculate the adjusted profit of Lydia Duarte for the year ended 30 September 20-5 by completing the table below.

	Effect on profit £	£
Profit for the year		25,000
1. Wages owing		
2. Rent paid in advance		
3. Vehicle depreciation		
4. Inventory understated		
5. Loan repayment		
6. Bank transfer from trade receivable		
7. Irrecoverable debt written off		
Adjusted profit for the year		

(b) Prepare the statement of financial position of Lydia Duarte at 30 September 20-5, taking into account all of the information given above.

Lydia Duarte: Statement of Financial Position as at 30 September 20-5

	£	£

7.

Karen is a sole trader. The following information was extracted from her ledger accounts at 1 January 20-3:

		£
vehicles – at cost		74,000
– provision for depreciation		33,500
machinery – at cost		37,000
– provision for depreciation		12,250

Karen's depreciation policies are:

- vehicles are depreciated at a rate of 30% per year using the reducing balance method
- machinery is depreciated at a rate of 20% per year on cost using the straight-line method

There were no purchases or sales of vehicles and machinery during the year ended 31 December 20-3.

(a) Calculate the amount of depreciation on:

(i) vehicles

(ii) machinery

to be included in the income statement for the year ended 31 December 20-3.

(b) Show the statement of financial position (extract) at 31 December 20-3 for:

(i) vehicles

(ii) machinery

8. Explain the treatment of the following in financial statements:

(a) Private expenses

....
....
....
....
....

(b) Goods for owner's use

....
....
....
....
....

(c) Goods on sale or return sent to a customer

....
....
....
....
....

FINANCIAL ACCOUNTING

QUESTIONS

CHAPTER 13: BUSINESS ORGANISATIONS AND FINANCING

1. Erica owns a shop selling children's clothes. She is a sole trader. She is considering converting her business to a private limited company with herself as the only shareholder.

Explain **two** advantages and **two** disadvantages, to Erica, of converting her business to a private limited company.

Advantages

....

....

....

....

....

....

....

Disadvantages

....

....

....

....

....

....

....

2.

> Jane and Scott are proposing to start a new business together which requires capital of £70,000. Jane and Scott can contribute £15,000 each.
> There is a good chance of making significant profits, but there is also a chance that the business could fail. A friend has advised that they form a private limited company.

Discuss **two** reasons why Jane and Scott should **not** form a private limited company.

3. Ann, Bee and Cat are planning to form a partnership. Their business will require capital of £120,000.

The partners are considering three possible ratios in which to make their capital contributions. Complete the table below with the amounts each partner will contribute based on each of the three ratios.

	Ann	Bee	Cat
Ratio of 1 : 1 : 1			
Ratio of 1 : 2 : 1			
Ratio of 2 : 2 : 1			

4. City Hotel Limited is a small private company that owns a medium range hotel in the city centre.

The company has an issued share capital of 500,000 £1 ordinary shares, all of which are owned by the four directors.

The company has the opportunity of buying the premises next door, currently used as a 'bed and breakfast' guest house, at a cost of £1m. City Hotel Limited would like to expand into the next door premises to create a larger hotel. The rooms next door will require refurbishment and some structural alterations. The directors seek your advice on two issues:

1. How to finance the purchase of new premises.
2. How to fund the refurbishment and alteration costs of the next door premises.

Issue 1

For the purchase of the next door premises at a cost of £1m, the accountant of City Hotel Limited suggests that 70% of the cost could be financed through a commercial mortgage for 15 years at a rate of 5% per annum.

Issue 2

The accountant has prepared budgeted financial statements for the next six months, based upon carrying out the refurbishment and alterations at an agreed cost within two months and having the 'new' rooms available for guest bookings for the following four months. The statements show the need for a maximum overdrawn bank balance of £40,000 at the end of month 2, reducing to £25,000 by the end of month 6, and then continuing to reduce for the remaining six months of the financial year.

The accountant advises that a bank overdraft facility should be arranged for twelve months – interest would be charged at a rate of 7% per annum. The alternative would be a bank short-term loan for twelve months at an interest rate of 6%.

You are to evaluate potential sources of finance to:

(a) Finance the purchase of the next door premises.
(b) Solve the funding of the refurbishment and alteration costs.

(a) **Purchase of the next door premises**

(b) **Funding the refurbishment and alteration costs**

CHAPTER 14: ACCOUNTING CONCEPTS AND INVENTORY VALUATION

1. (a) Explain the following **two** accounting concepts:

   (i) Prudence

   (ii) Consistency

(b) Explain the importance of applying these **two** accounting concepts when preparing the financial statements of a business.

....

....

....

....

....

....

....

....

....

....

2. When a business depreciates non-current assets it applies a number of accounting concepts. Which one of the following pairs is applied?

A	Materiality; business entity	
B	Prudence; consistency	
C	Going concern; accruals	
D	Realisation; money measurement	

3.

Tanya runs a clothing store which sells 'designer' beachwear. At 31 December 20-4, her financial year-end, there are 100 items of the 'Ripcurl' beachwear range left unsold. These had been bought in the spring at a cost of £15 each and Tanya had expected to sell them for £30 each. As there will be changes in the range for next year, these will have to be reduced to a price of £17.50 each. However, in order to sell them Tanya will have to pay extra advertising costs totalling £300.

(a) Calculate the value of the remaining 'Ripcurl' beachwear range to be included in the closing inventory value at 31 December 20-4.

....

....

....

....

....

....

(b) State the main accounting concept that is applied to the valuation of inventory.

....

4. A business has some closing inventory that has been damaged. The cost of the inventory was £850. It can be repaired at a cost of £200 and will then be sold for £950.

What is the value of this closing inventory?

A	£650	
B	£750	
C	£850	
D	£950	

5.

Here4U Ltd owns and operates a number of convenience food shops. The trainee accountant has prepared a draft income statement for the year ended 30 June 20-4. She is unsure of the treatment of the following.

(1) Tickett & Run Certified Accountants audit the financial statements and give tax advice. Their fee for the year ended 30 June 20-4 is estimated to be £7,500. This has not been included in the draft income statement.

(2) Part of one shop is rented out to a dry cleaning business. Here4U Ltd is owed rent of £1,500 at 30 June 20-4. This has not been included in the draft financial statements.

(3) Here4U Ltd purchased new shop tills costing £35,000 during the year. These have been included in non-current assets, but depreciation at a rate of 20% per year on cost using the straight-line method has not yet been allowed for.

(4) Included in the closing inventory was tinned goods at a cost price of £1,000. They would normally sell for £1,800. However, the tins are damaged and can only be sold for £800.

(5) The trade receivables figure at 30 June 20-4 is £10,500. Included in this amount is £2,000 owed by Trade Caterers Ltd which has gone into liquidation. The accountant of Here4U Ltd is certain that this amount will not be paid.

Complete the table below. For each item, state the most relevant accounting concept and the effect any adjustment would have on the profit for the year.

Item	Effect on profit	Concept
(1) Fee for audit and tax advice		
(2) Rent		
(3) Depreciation		
(4) Inventory		
(5) Irrecoverable debt		

CHAPTER 15: FURTHER ASPECTS OF FINANCIAL STATEMENTS

1. The following information is available about commission received for the year ended 30 September 20-4:

	£
Debit balance brought forward on 1 October 20-3	185
Receipts during year ended 30 September 20-4	3,045
Debit balance brought down on 1 October 20-4	260

    How much should be shown as commission income in the income statement for the year ended 30 September 20-4?

A	£3,305	
B	£3,120	
C	£3,490	
D	£2,970	

2. A debt which was written off as irrecoverable last year has been recovered this year. What effect will the recovery of an irrecoverable debt have on this year's profit, current assets, and bank balance of the business?

	Profit for the year	Current assets	Bank balance	
A	Decrease	Decrease	Increase	
B	Decrease	No effect	Increase	
C	Increase	Decrease	No effect	
D	Increase	Increase	Increase	

3. A business has a policy of maintaining its provision for doubtful debts at 5 per cent of trade receivables. The provision at the start of the financial year is £950. At the end of the financial year trade receivables are £20,000. What effect will any change in provision for doubtful debts have on this year's profit, current assets, and bank balance of the business?

	Profit for the year	Current assets	Bank balance	
A	Increase £50	Decrease £50	No effect	
B	No effect	Increase £50	Decrease £50	
C	Decrease £50	Decrease £50	No effect	
D	Decrease £950	No effect	Increase £50	

4.

> Lily's trade receivables at 31 October 20-8 were £21,040.
>
> The provision for doubtful debts at 1 November 20-7 was £550.80.
>
> She has been advised that she should adjust the provision for doubtful debts to 3% of trade receivables at 31 October 20-8.

(a) Calculate the provision for doubtful debts at 31 October 20-8.

....

....

....

....

....

(b) Calculate the effect the change in the provision will have on Lily's profit for the year ended 31 October 20-8.

....

....

....

....

....

(c) Calculate the net amount of trade receivables to be shown in Lily's statement of financial position at 31 October 20-8.

....

....

....

....

....

5. A business has recently sold a computer system which had a net book value (carrying amount) of £1,000. The provision for depreciation on the computer at the time of sale was £2,500. The sale proceeds, £350, were received by bank transfer.

You are to complete the computer disposal account:

Dr		Computer Disposal Account		Cr
	£		£

6.

Amy is a sole trader. The following information was extracted from her ledger accounts at 1 July 20-6:

	£
Vehicles at cost	46,000
Provision for depreciation	22,000

During the financial year ended 30 June 20-7, Amy sold a vehicle for £6,500. This vehicle had originally cost £12,000 and had been depreciated by £5,250. Amy also purchased a new vehicle costing £16,250.

Amy depreciates vehicles at the rate of 25% per year using the reducing balance method. Depreciation is calculated on vehicles held at the end of the financial year.

(a) Calculate the profit or loss on sale of the vehicle which has been sold.

....

....

....

....

....

(b) Calculate the depreciation on vehicles to be included in the income statement for the year ended 30 June 20-7.

....

....

....

....

....

7. At the end of his financial year on 31 December 20-8 Sam Mehta, the owner of a business, was preparing financial statements.

The following information had yet to be recorded in the general ledger of Sam's business.

At 31 December 20-8:

- Inventory is valued at £14,050.
- Depreciation is to be provided on vehicles at 20% per annum using the reducing balance method. The debit balance on vehicles at cost account on 31 December 20-8 is £40,000.
- The provision for doubtful debts is to be maintained at 4% of trade receivables; at the year end trade receivables totalled £16,400.
- Rent income, £540, is due but unpaid.
- Vehicle expenses, £250, are prepaid.

You are to record the information in the ledger accounts shown below. Balance the accounts at 31 December 20-8.

GENERAL LEDGER

Dr			Inventory Account				Cr
20-8			£	20-8			£
Jan	1	Balance b/d	12,240				

Dr			Provision for Depreciation (Vehicles) Account				Cr
20-8			£	20-8			£
				Jan	1	Balance b/d	14,400

Dr				Provision for Doubtful Debts Account			Cr
20-8			£	20-8			£
				Jan	1	Balance b/d	720

Dr				Rent Income Account			Cr
20-8			£	20-8			£
Jan	1	Balance b/d	220	Jan-Dec		Bank	4,180

Dr				Vehicle Expenses Account			Cr
20-8			£	20-8			£
Jan-Dec		Bank	3,230	Jan	1	Balance b/d	170

8. Alex Munro owns an estate agency. He provides the following information for the year ended 30 April 20-3:

	£
Salaries	33,470
Drawings	16,950
Irrecoverable debts	255
Administration expenses	24,075
Discount allowed	315
Recovery of irrecoverable debts	195
Rent income	2,360
Fee income for the year	86,245

Additional information	As at 1 May 20-2 £	As at 30 April 20-3 £
Provision for depreciation of non-current assets	25,000	27,500
Provision for doubtful debts	460	310
Rent income paid in advance	–	540

During the year ended 30 April 20-3, a vehicle which had originally cost £12,000 was sold for £3,750. The depreciation on the vehicle was £7,500.

Prepare the income statement of Alex Munro for the year ended 30 April 20-3.

9.

Tamsin Smith owns a retail business. She has calculated the gross profit for the year ended 30 June 20-4 as £14,760.

She has a computerised system of inventory control, which automatically updates the inventory records whenever a sale is made. The closing inventory value from the computer system of £10,330 was used in the calculation of gross profit.

On 30 June 20-4, a physical inventory take was carried out and the inventory was valued at £9,760.

The following balances have been extracted from the books of account at 30 June 20-4.

	£
Vehicles – at cost	32,000
– provision for depreciation	14,000
Shop fittings – at cost	17,000
– provision for depreciation	6,800
Trade receivables	8,310
Provision for doubtful debts	245
Operating expenses	6,240
Rent income	5,600

Adjustments have yet to be made for the following:

(1) Rent income paid in advance at 30 June 20-4 is £650.

(2) Operating expenses owing at 30 June 20-4 is £495.

(3) During the year, recovery of irrecoverable debts is £220.

(4) At 30 June 20-4, irrecoverable debts to be written off is £590.

(5) Vehicles are depreciated at a rate of 25% per year using the reducing balance method.

(6) Shop fittings are depreciated at a rate of 20% per year on cost using the straight-line method.

(7) Tamsin's policy is to maintain the provision for doubtful debts at 2.5% of trade receivables.

Required:

Prepare Tamsin's income statement for the year ended 30 June 20-4.

CHAPTER 16: PREPARING SOLE TRADER FINANCIAL STATEMENTS

1. Anton Buszczak owns a retail business. He provides the following balances from his books for the year ended 30 June 20-6:

	£
Purchases	59,450
Revenue (Sales)	145,630
Inventory at 1 July 20-5	4,525
Vehicle running expenses	3,965
Rent and business rates	12,080
Office expenses	6,335
Discount allowed	580
Wages and salaries	43,190
Machinery – cost	25,000
– provision for depreciation	11,000
Vehicles – cost	33,000
– provision for depreciation	12,200
Trade receivables	4,155
Trade payables	10,845
Capital	28,550
Drawings	12,580
Cash at bank	3,365

   Adjustments have yet to be made for the following:

   (1) Closing inventory of £5,385.

   (2) Office expenses owing £345.

   (3) Vehicle running expenses prepaid £175.

   (4) Depreciation of machinery for the year £4,000.

   (5) Depreciation of vehicles for the year £8,500.

Required:

Prepare the income statement of Anton Buszczak for the year ended 30 June 20-6, together with his statement of financial position at that date.

Continue on a separate sheet

2. The following balances have been extracted from the books of Samantha Martinez at 30 September 20-4:

	£	£
Capital		160,500
Revenue (Sales)		245,084
Purchases	156,027	
Office salaries	50,133	
Business rates and insurances	6,433	
Administration expenses	17,122	
Irrecoverable debts	295	
Provision for doubtful debts 1 October 20-3		645
Recovery of irrecoverable debts		176
Property at cost	220,000	
Office equipment at cost	45,000	
Provisions for depreciation 1 October 20-3:		
Property		39,600
Office equipment		16,500
Trade receivables and Trade payables	18,400	13,125
Inventory at 1 October 20-3	5,893	
Drawings	22,150	

Additional information at 30 September 20-4 not yet included by Samantha:

(1) Closing inventory £7,541.

(2) Office salaries owing £510.

(3) Insurance prepaid £232.

(4) During the year, Samantha took goods to the value of £750 from the business for her private use.

(5) Samantha maintains a provision for doubtful debts of 3% of trade receivables outstanding at the year end.

(6) Samantha provides for depreciation of non-current assets as follows:
    property at 2% per year on cost using the straight-line method;
    office equipment 25% per year using the reducing balance method.

Required:

(a) Prepare Samantha's income statement for the year ended 30 September 20-4.

(b) Prepare an extract from Samantha's statement of financial position as at 30 September 20-4 showing the capital section only.

Chapter 16

3.

Charlotte Lee is preparing the financial statements for her business for the year ended 31 December 20-5. The trading section of the income statement shows a gross profit of £67,386.

Charlotte Lee has extracted the following balances from the business books of account in order to complete the income statement:

	£
Rent income	7,864
Irrecoverable debts	245
Operating expenses	32,149
Wages	40,231
Fixtures and fittings at cost (1 January 20-5)	18,300
Vehicle at cost (1 January 20-5)	15,000
Provision for depreciation – vehicle (1 January 20-5)	5,400
Trade receivables (31 December 20-5)	24,200
Provision for doubtful debts (1 January 20-5)	810

Additional information

(1) Included in Charlotte Lee's closing inventory are goods which cost £400. These have been damaged and will have to be destroyed.

(2) Charlotte has taken goods for her own use from the business. The goods cost £620 and would have been sold for £1,120.

(3) Charlotte rents part of her property to another business and she has been prepaid January's rent of £620 at 31 December 20-5.

(4) Included in the total for operating expenses is £295 paid for the year ended 31 December 20-6 and a payment of £6,500 for the purchase of fixtures.

(5) Wages for the final week of December 20-4 amounting to £456 had not been paid at 31 December 20-5.

(6) Charlotte sold the vehicle on 30 April 20-5. She received £7,950. She had purchased the vehicle on 1 January 20-3. It is her policy to depreciate the vehicle using the reducing balance method at the rate of 20% per annum. A full year's depreciation is charged in the year of disposal.

(7) Fixtures and fittings are depreciated using the straight-line method at the rate of 20% per annum on cost.

(8) It is Charlotte's policy to maintain the provision for doubtful debts at 4% of trade receivables.

Required:

Prepare the income statement for Charlotte Lee's business for the year ended 31 December 20-5.

4.

The following trial balance has been extracted from the books of account of Henry Dunstone, a sole trader, at 31 March 20-7:

	£	£
Bank		4,107
Capital at 1 April 20-6		103,856
Discounts	862	741
Drawings	10,124	
Fixtures and fittings at cost	30,400	
Fixtures and fittings – provision for depreciation		9,120
Inventory at 1 April 20-6	33,940	
Machinery at cost	55,500	
Machinery – provision for depreciation		19,980
Operating expenses	35,336	
Provision for doubtful debts		1,045
Purchases and Revenue (Sales)	136,240	283,135
Rent and business rates	18,022	
Returns	1,068	
Salaries	93,085	
Trade receivables and Trade payables	57,240	49,833
	471,817	471,817

Additional information

(1) Inventory at 31 March 20-7 is valued at £36,875.

(2) During the year ended 31 March 20-7, Henry Dunstone had taken £1,475 of goods for his own use.

(3) At 31 March 20-7, salaries due and unpaid are £1,465.

(4) Rent paid for the period 1 April 20-7 to 30 June 20-7 is £1,950.

(5) The provision for doubtful debts is to be 2.5% of trade receivables at 31 March 20-7.

(6) Depreciation on machinery is to be provided using the reducing balance method at 20% per annum.

(7) Depreciation on fixtures and fittings is to be provided using the straight-line method at 15% per annum on cost.

Required:

Prepare the income statement of Henry Dunstone for the year ended 31 March 20-7, together with his statement of financial position at that date.

CHAPTER 17: FINANCIAL STATEMENTS OF LIMITED COMPANIES

1. What does the term 'limited' mean in the name of a company?

A	The shareholders do not have any voting rights at the annual general meeting of the company	
B	The company is a public limited company	
C	In the event of insolvency of the company, ordinary shareholders are paid off before debenture holders	
D	The company is a private limited company	

2. Indicate the heading under which the following items will be shown in a limited company's statement of financial position.

   Choose from the following headings: Non-current assets, Current assets, Current liabilities, Non-current liabilities, Issued share capital, Capital reserve, Revenue reserve.

Item	Heading
Tax liabilities	
Share premium	
Buildings	
Retained earnings	
Ordinary shares	
Debentures (repayable in five years' time)	

3.

The equity section of the statement of financial position of Axiom plc at 30 June 20-4 is shown below:

Equity	£
Ordinary shares of £1 each fully paid	600,000
Share premium	90,000
Retained earnings	330,000
	1,020,000

On 1 January 20-5, the directors issued 150,000 new ordinary shares at a price of £1.60 each. The issue was fully subscribed.

During the year ended 30 June 20-5, dividends paid totalled £220,000.

The profit for the year ended 30 June 20-5 was £365,000.

Prepare the statement of changes in equity of Axiom plc for the year ended 30 June 20-5. Use the table provided.

Axiom plc

Statement of Changes in Equity for the year ended 30 June 20-5

	Issued share capital £	Share premium £	Retained earnings £	Total £
At 1 July 20-4	600,000	90,000	330,000	1,020,000
Issue of shares				
Profit for the year				
Dividends paid				
At 30 June 20-5				

4.

The equity section of the statement of financial position of Bohan Ltd at 1 January 20-2 is shown below:

Equity	£
Ordinary shares of 50p each fully paid	220,000
Retained earnings	118,000
	338,000

On 1 November 20-2, the directors issued 220,000 new ordinary shares at a price of 80p per share. The issue was fully subscribed.

During the year ended 31 December 20-2, dividends paid totalled £45,000.

The profit for the year ended 31 December 20-2 was £79,000.

Prepare the statement of changes in equity of Bohan Ltd for the year ended 31 December 20-2. Use the table provided.

Bohan Ltd
Statement of Changes in Equity for the year ended 31 December 20-2

	Issued share capital £	Share premium £	Retained earnings £	Total £
At 1 January 20-2	220,000	–	118,000	338,000
Issue of shares	110,000	66,000		176,000
Profit for the year			79,000	79,000
Dividends paid			(45,000)	(45,000)
At 31 December 20-2	330,000	66,000	152,000	548,000

5. (a) Define the term 'capital reserves'. Give an example of a capital reserve.

Definition ....

....

....

....

Example ....

....

....

....

(b) Define the term 'revenue reserves'. Give an example of a revenue reserve.

Definition ....

....

....

....

Example ....

....

....

....

6. The trading section of the income statement for Akram Ltd for the year ended 31 December 20-4 has been completed. It showed a gross profit of £148,800.

The following balances remained in the books of account of Akram Ltd at 31 December 20-4:

	£
Bank loan repayable 20-8	30,000
Ordinary shares of 50p each	100,000
Cash and cash equivalents	135,427
Inventory	25,364
Operating expenses	92,530
Loan interest paid	900
Non-current assets at cost	120,000
Provision for depreciation at 1 January 20-4	36,000
Trade payables	27,146
Trade receivables	38,196
Retained earnings	35,471
Share premium	10,000

Additional information:

- The bank loan was taken out last year and interest is payable at the rate of 6% per annum.
- It is the company policy to depreciate non-current assets using the reducing balance method at the rate of 30% per annum.
- The directors have been advised that there should be a provision for corporation tax for the year ended 31 December 20-4. It is estimated that this should be 20% of the profit before tax.
- On 15 December 20-4 the directors paid a dividend of 10p per share. Apart from in the bank account, this has not been recorded in the books of account.
- On 29 December 20-4 the directors issued 50,000 new ordinary shares at a price of 90p per share. The issue was fully subscribed and, apart from in the bank account, this has not been recorded in the books of account.

(a) Complete the income statement of Akram Ltd for the year ended 31 December 20-4.

AKRAM LTD
Income Statement for the year ended 31 December 20-4

	£	£
Gross profit		148,800
Expenses:		

(b) Prepare the statement of changes in equity of Akram Ltd for the year ended 31 December 20-4.

AKRAM LTD
Statement of Changes In Equity for the year ended 31 December 20-4

	Issued share capital £	Share premium £	Retained earnings £	Total £

(c) Prepare the statement of financial position of Akram Ltd as at 31 December 20-4.

AKRAM LTD
Statement of Financial Position as at 31 December 20-4

	£	£	£

7. The following is the summarised draft statement of financial position of Chapelporth Limited as at 30 September 20-6:

	Cost £000	Depreciation £000	Carrying amount £000
Non-current assets	2,000	800	1,200
Current assets		380	
Less Current liabilities		220	160
			1,360
Ordinary share capital			1,000
Retained earnings			360
			1,360

Depreciation has been charged on non-current assets at 20% for the year using the straight-line method.

After preparing the draft statement of financial position, the directors of Chapelporth Limited wish to incorporate the following in the financial statements:

(a) Vehicle expenses prepaid at the year end amounted to £3,000.

(b) Depreciation of non-current assets is to be charged at 25% for the year using the straight-line method.

(c) Closing inventory has been undervalued by £10,000.

(d) Corporation tax of £40,000 is to be paid on the year's profit.

Required

Using the table below show the effect, ie increase/decrease/no change, and state the amount that any amendments resulting from notes (a) to (d) above will have on the profit for the year and the statement of financial position of Chapelporth Limited.

Note	Profit for the year	Retained earnings	Total equity	Current assets	Current liabilities
(a)					
(b)					
(c)					
(d)					

CHAPTER 18: FINANCIAL RATIOS

1.
Samantha owns a clothes shop. She is concerned that her closing inventory is much higher than her opening inventory and that the business is becoming inefficient. Last year, her rate of inventory turnover was eight times.

She provides the following extract from her income statement for the current year:

	£	£
Revenue		117,950
Opening inventory	10,350	
Purchases	77,550	
Closing inventory	14,150	
Cost of sales		73,750
Gross profit		44,200

Required:

(a) Calculate the rate of inventory turnover for the current year. State the formula used.

Formula

....

....

....

Calculation

....

....

....

....

....

(b) Comment on the change in the rate of inventory turnover and explain to Samantha whether or not her business is becoming less efficient.

....

....

....

....

....

....

....

2. Tick the boxes to indicate which of the following current assets and current liabilities will be included in the calculation of:

- the current ratio
- the liquid capital ratio

	Current ratio	Liquid capital ratio
Trade payables		
Inventory		
Tax liabilities		
Other payables		

3.

The directors of Capper Ltd are concerned that, despite making a profit for the year of £150,220, the company has a large bank overdraft. The following information has been taken from the financial statements at the year end:

	£
Closing inventory	105,630
Trade receivables	162,940
Bank overdraft	77,620
Trade payables	134,230

Required:

(a) (i) Calculate the current ratio. State the formula used.

Formula

....

....

Calculation

....

....

....

....

(ii) Calculate the liquid capital ratio. State the formula used.

Formula

....

....

Calculation

....

....

....

....

(b) Evaluate the liquidity position of Capper Ltd as shown by the current ratio and the liquid capital ratio. The industry average ratios are: current ratio 1.8:1; liquid capital ratio 0.9:1.

(c) Explain to the directors of Capper Ltd how it is possible for a business to make a profit but still have an overdraft.

4.

The directors of Burlington Ltd are concerned about the profitability of the business. The income statement for the year ended 30 June 20-6 is shown below.

Burlington Ltd
Income Statement for the year ended 30 June 20-6

	£	£
Revenue		240,000
Opening inventory	22,000	
Purchases	172,000	
Less Closing inventory	26,000	
Cost of sales		168,000
Gross profit		72,000
Less Expenses:		
Wages	34,300	
Advertising	11,750	
Depreciation	13,950	
		60,000
Profit from operations		12,000
Less Finance costs		2,400
Profit for the year before tax		9,600

Required:

(a) Calculate the gross profit margin. State the formula used.

Formula

....

....

Calculation

....

....

(b) Calculate the profit in relation to revenue percentage. State the formula used.

Formula

....

....

Calculation

....

....

....

....

(c) Calculate the rate of inventory turnover. State the formula used.

Formula

....

....

Calculation

....

....

....

....

(d) Discuss the actions which the directors of Burlington Ltd could take to improve each of the ratios calculated in (a) to (c). Explain any problems that these actions might cause the business.

5.

The directors of Friel Ltd are assessing the liquidity of the company. In particular they are concerned about the credit they give to their customers. At the same time their suppliers are pressing for earlier settlement of amounts due. Both of these are having an adverse effect on the company's bank balance.

The following information has been taken from the financial statements at the year end:

	£
Credit sales for the year	357,700
Credit purchases for the year	258,775
Trade receivables	34,300
Trade payables	27,650

Required:

(a) (i) Calculate the trade receivable days. State the formula used.

Formula

....

....

Calculation

....

....

(ii) Calculate the trade payable days. State the formula used.

Formula

....

....

Calculation

....

....

(b) Evaluate the liquidity position of Friel Ltd as shown by the trade receivable and trade payable days. The industry average ratios are: trade receivables = 37 days; trade payables = 33 days.

MANAGEMENT ACCOUNTING
QUESTIONS

CHAPTER 19: BUDGETING AND BUDGETARY CONTROL

1. Which of the following statements apply better to either incremental budgeting or zero-based budgeting?

Statements	Incremental budgeting	Zero-based budgeting
The budget 'starts from scratch'		
Inefficiencies and overspending are identified and avoided		
An increase is applied to last period's budget figures		
The budget may include continuing activities that are uneconomic		

2. C & B Limited is a manufacturer of curtains and blinds. The business has developed over the years since it was formed as a sole trader business by Jayne Yadav, who is the company's managing director. There are ten employees and annual sales revenue is approximately £2,000,000 per year.

   Jayne wishes to implement a system of budgeting into the business.

   Required:

   (a) Explain the key benefits of budgeting to Jayne Yadav.

   (b) Explain the limitations of budgets to Jayne Yadav.

   (c) Explain how managers can use budgets to control the business.

3. Indicate whether the following statements are favourable or adverse variances.

Statements	Favourable variance	Adverse variance
Budgeted revenue £35,000; actual revenue £34,000		
Actual costs £15,500; budgeted costs £16,000		
Budgeted profit £46,000; actual profit £47,000		
Budgeted costs £12,000; actual costs £11,500		

4. The income statement for the year ended 31 December 20-3 of James Martland, who sells a single product online, was:

	£	£
Revenue (240,000 units)		3,600,000
Opening inventory (20,000 units)	120,000	
Add Purchases (238,000 units)	1,666,000	
Less Closing inventory (18,000 units)	126,000	
Cost of sales		1,660,000
Gross profit		1,940,000
Less Expenses:		
Wages	420,000	
General expenses	345,000	
Rent	225,000	
Depreciation	200,000	
Carriage outwards (£0.75 per unit)	180,000	
		1,370,000
Profit for the year		570,000

Additional information for the year ending 31 December 20-4:

1. The unit selling price will increase by 10%. This is expected to decrease the number of sales units by 5%.
2. The supplier has announced a rise of 4% on last year's price.
3. The ratio of units of closing inventory to sales units will be the same in both years. Closing inventory is to be valued at the cost price for the year.
4. Wages are expected to increase by 6.0%.
5. General expenses are expected to increase by 1%.
6. Rent is fixed for the year at £225,000.
7. 25 per cent reducing balance depreciation for the year is to be calculated on the second year of ownership of non-current assets with a cost price of £800,000.
8. Carriage outwards will, because of inflation, increase to £0.90 per unit sold.

Required:

Prepare the budgeted income statement for James Martland for the year ending 31 December 20-4, taking into account the changes identified.

James Martland
Budgeted Income Statement for the year ending 31 December 20-4

	£	£

Workings:

5. The statement of financial position of Sylwia Sipkova as at 31 December 20-5 was:

	£	£
Non-current Assets		150,000
Less depreciation for the year		30,000
Net book value		120,000
Current Assets		
Inventory	30,000	
Trade receivables	65,000	
Bank	10,000	
	105,000	
Less Current Liabilities		
Trade payables	60,000	
Net Current Assets		45,000
NET ASSETS		165,000
FINANCED BY		
Capital		
Opening capital		144,000
Add Profit for the year		46,000
Less Drawings		25,000
		165,000

Sylwia Sipkova asks for your assistance in preparing her budgeted statement of financial position as at 31 December 20-6. She has identified the following changes compared to the actual results, above, as at 31 December 20-5:

1. Currently, trade receivables take, on average, two months to pay. Sylwia intends to reduce this to one-and-a-half months.
2. Currently, Sylwia pays trade payables, on average, after three months. Her suppliers now require her to pay after two months.
3. During the year, Sylwia plans to take drawings of £35,000 from the business bank account.

You note the following from Sylwia's budgeted income statement for 20-6:
- all sales and purchases are made on credit
- revenue £432,000
- purchases £294,000
- closing inventory is one-and-a-half month's purchases
- expenses £107,500 (this includes the amount for depreciation, being the second year reducing balance on the non-current assets)

(a) Prepare the budgeted statement of financial position of Sylwia Sipkova as at 31 December 20-6, taking into account the changes identified.

Sylwia Sipkova
Budgeted Statement of Financial Position as at 31 December 20-6

	£	£

Workings:

(b) Show your calculation of the budgeted closing bank balance as at 31 December 20-6.

CHAPTER 20: MARGINAL COSTING AND BREAK-EVEN

1. Which one of the following is the correct method for calculating contribution?

A	Sales revenue minus variable costs	
B	Sales revenue minus fixed costs	
C	Sales revenue divided by fixed costs	
D	Sales revenue plus variable costs	

2. Choose the correct description for each of the three terms in the table below.

Select your entries for the 'Description' column from the following list:

The cost of producing one extra unit of output

Break-even units x selling price per unit

A fixed cost that increases by a large amount all at once

Sales revenue minus variable costs

The point at which there is neither a profit nor a loss

The point at which selling price equals variable costs

Contribution plus fixed costs

Cost where a part is variable and a part is fixed

Cost that does not normally change when the level of output changes

Sales returns minus variable costs

Costs where the cost per unit increases as output increases

Costs where the total cost varies in proportion with output

Contribution minus fixed costs

Term	Description
Profit or loss	
Variable costs	
Break-even revenue	

3. A business has forecast its internet expense for the year to be £900. This consists of a fixed element which is ⅓ of the total cost; the remaining ⅔ are variable based on internet usage. Another internet supplier offers to reduce the fixed element by ½, but the variable cost of usage will increase by 20%.

   How much will the forecast internet expense be from the other supplier, assuming internet usage does not change?

A	£540	
B	£870	
C	£1,020	
D	£1,160	

4. Clark Limited makes a product which is coded CL18. The selling price of product CL18 is £15 per unit and the total variable cost is £10 per unit. Clark Limited estimates that the fixed costs per quarter associated with this product are £2,000.

   (a) Calculate the break-even point, in units per quarter, for product CL18.

   ☐ units

   (b) Calculate the estimated profit, in £ per quarter, if Clark Limited makes and sells 550 units of product CL18.

   £ ☐

5. The following is the break-even chart of a business which makes and sells a single product.

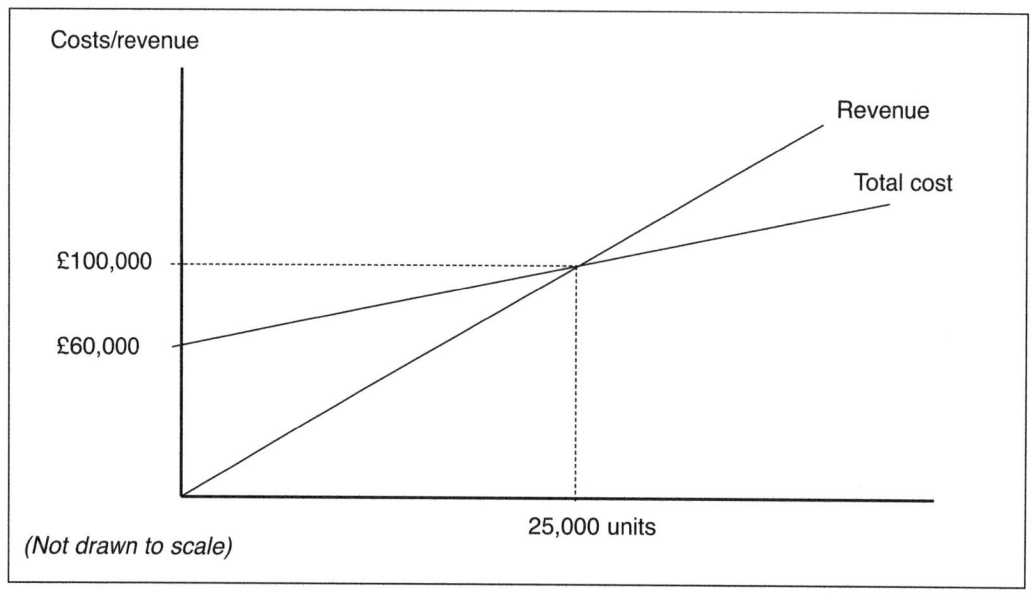

(Not drawn to scale)

(a) Calculate the selling price per unit of the product.

....
....
....

(b) Calculate the variable cost per unit.

....
....
....

(c) State the formula used to calculate contribution per unit.

....
....
....

(d) Calculate the contribution per unit.

....

....

....

(e) Calculate the forecast profit if 35,000 units are manufactured and sold.

....

....

....

6. Nikko Limited has made the following estimates for next month:

Selling price	£20 per unit
Variable cost	£15 per unit
Fixed costs for the month	£100,000
Budgeted output	25,000 units
Maximum output	35,000 units

As an accounts assistant, you are to carry out the following tasks:

(a) Calculate:

The break-even point in units next month	
The break-even point in sales revenue next month	
The estimated profit if 30,000 units are made and sold next month	

(b) Calculate the profit at:

The budgeted output for next month	
The maximum output for next month	

7. Wyvern Limited makes a product which is numbered WV5. The selling price of product WV5 is £28 per unit and the total variable cost is £16 per unit. Wyvern Limited estimates that the fixed costs per quarter associated with this product are £24,000.

   (a) Calculate the break-even point, in units per quarter, for product WV5.

   ☐ units

   (b) Calculate the break-even sales revenue, in £ per quarter, for product WV5.

   £ ☐

   (c) Calculate the estimated profit, in £ per quarter, if Wyvern Limited makes and sells 3,500 units of product WV5.

   £ ☐

   (d) If Wyvern Limited increases the selling price of WV5 by £1, what will be the impact on the break-even point, assuming no change in the number of units sold?

The break-even point will decrease	
The break-even point will stay the same	
The break-even point will increase	

8. Boxster Limited makes boxes for customers in the food and drink industry. The company has prepared a budget for the next quarter for one of its boxes, BB4. This budget is based on producing and selling 1,000 units.

One of the customers of Boxster Limited has indicated that it may be significantly increasing its order level for box BB4 for the next quarter and it appears that activity levels of 1,200 units and 2,000 units are feasible.

Complete the table below and calculate the budgeted total profit of BB4 at the different activity levels.

Batches produced and sold	1,000	1,200	2,000
	£	£	£
Revenue	35,000	42,000	70,000
Variable costs:			
• Direct materials	7,500	9,000	15,000
• Direct labour	10,500	12,600	21,000
• Overheads	6,000	7,200	12,000
Semi-variable costs:			
• Variable element	1,500	1,800	3,000
• Fixed element	3,000	3,000	3,000
Total cost	28,500	33,600	54,000
Total profit	6,500	8,400	16,000

CHAPTER 21: DECISION-MAKING SITUATIONS

1. A profitable business has spare capacity. If it makes additional sales it can increase its profits when:

A	The selling price is above marginal cost	
B	The selling price is below marginal cost	
C	The selling price is the same as marginal cost	
D	The total cost is below marginal cost	

2. A business makes a single product. The selling price of the product is £40 and the marginal cost of the product is £25. A customer offers to buy 1,000 units of the product at a price of £30. If this offer is accepted the profits of the business:

A	Will increase by £5,000	
B	Will decrease by £5,000	
C	Will increase by £30,000	
D	Will be unchanged	

3. Mercia Airways is a local airline which flies to short-haul destinations within the UK and Europe. The costs of weekly flight MA 005 to Rome, which uses a 100 seater aircraft are as follows:

>   Direct materials   £15.00 per passenger
>   Direct labour   £10.00 per passenger
>   Fixed overheads   £3,500 per flight

For next week's flight, sixty seats have been sold at a standard-class fare of £100 each.

Required:

(a) Calculate the total cost per seat on this flight with sixty seats sold.

(b) Calculate the marginal cost per seat.

(c) Calculate the profit or loss if no further tickets are sold for this flight.

(d) Refer to the text on the next page and advise the marketing manager whether either of the two suggested possibilities should be considered; explain your reasoning, and illustrate your answer with income statements.

The marketing manager thinks it unlikely that any further standard-class fares will be sold. There are two possibilities that she must consider:

- to release the surplus seats to a firm that sells cheap flights: the airline will receive £45 for each seat sold and, from past experience, the marketing manager expects thirty seats to be sold

- to sell all forty spare seats to a local newspaper, which will offer them as prizes for a competition: the newspaper will pay £35 per seat

4. The Last Company Ltd is famous for its 'Snowdon' range of hill-walking boots. The management of the company is considering the production for next year and has asked for help with certain financial decisions.

The following information is available:

Wholesale selling price (per pair)	£60
Direct materials (per pair)	£20
Direct labour (per pair)	£18
Fixed overheads	£200,000 per year

The company is planning to manufacture 12,500 pairs of boots next year.

Required:

(a) You are to calculate:

- the total cost per pair
- the marginal cost per pair
- the profit or loss if 12,500 pairs of boots are sold

(b) An internet sales company, Zambesi Ltd, has approached The Last Company Ltd with a view to selling the 'Snowdon' boot through its website. Zambesi Ltd offers two contracts:

- either 2,500 pairs of boots at £45 per pair
- or 5,000 pairs of boots at £37 per pair

As The Last Company Ltd usually sells through specialist shops, it is not expected that 'normal' sales will be affected. These 'special orders' are within the capacity of the factory, and fixed overheads will remain unchanged.

You are to advise the management whether these offers should be accepted. Illustrate your answer with income statements.

Continue on a separate sheet

5. SecureWaste Limited manufactures and sells specialist waste bins used in hospitals. The waste bins have a selling price of £275 per unit and, in the current year, the company expects to sell 6,000 units.

The variable costs per unit are:

	£
Material C: 22 kilos at £3 per kilo	66.00
Material D: 2.5 litres at £6 per litre	15.00
Skilled labour: 2 hours at £20.00 per hour	40.00
Semi-skilled labour: 3 hours at £15.00 per hour	45.00
Total variable cost per unit	166.00

Budgeted fixed overheads for the current year are £355,400 and the budgeted profit for the year is £298,600.

SecureWaste Limited has received an enquiry from a potential overseas customer. This customer wishes to place an order for 1,500 units if a total sales price of £330,000 is agreed and delivery takes place within four months, which is before the end of SecureWaste Limited's financial year. The potential customer is prepared to pay in full using bank guaranteed systems once SecureWaste Limited presents shipping and insurance documents for the order, the costs of which must be paid by SecureWaste Limited, expected to be £14,500.

If the potential overseas customer is satisfied with quality standards and delivery terms there is the expectation that future orders will be placed for around 2,500 units each year.

In considering these orders, the following information may be useful:

- The directors of SecureWaste Limited have been looking to develop overseas sales.
- For the current year, skilled labour is forecast to be under-utilised by 550 hours. It is intended to retain the skilled labour in the company and to continue paying them for the company's standard 35-hour week.
- Any shortfall in skilled labour hours would be worked as overtime at a premium of £10 per hour, paid in addition to the hourly rate.
- The wages of non-production employees are included within fixed overheads.
- Additional materials and semi-skilled labour at current prices and rates are readily available.

You are required to evaluate the financial and non-financial implications of the proposed order from the overseas customer. Include a justified recommendation as to whether the order should be accepted or rejected.

6. A company uses cost-plus pricing for its price setting. The total cost of each unit it makes is £8.50. The selling price is set at 160% of the total cost per unit.

   What is (i) profit per unit, and (ii) selling price per unit?

A	(i) £5.10	(ii) £13.60	
B	(i) £5.10	(ii) £8.50	
C	(i) £8.50	(ii) £13.60	
D	(i) £8.50	(ii) £5.10	

7. Oakdene Limited manufactures its 'Malvern' table and chairs sets.

   The company currently produces 250 of its 'Malvern' sets each month.

   The costs per set are:

   Materials: 5 kilos @ £20 per kilo

   Labour: 5 hours @ £15 per hour

   Total fixed costs are £26,250 monthly.

   The company uses cost-plus pricing and the selling price is set at 160% of the total cost per set.

   If production exceeds 300 sets in any one month, overtime will be paid at a rate of £25 per hour for each extra labour hour worked.

   The company has received an order from a new customer. This order will increase total production for each of the following months to 375 sets.

   Required:

   (a) Calculate the total cost per set if the order is accepted and 375 sets are produced.

   (b) Calculate the change between the new selling price and the original selling.

8. Wyvern Porcelain Limited produces decorated porcelain figures which are sold in quality shops both in the UK and abroad. The figures are especially popular with holidaymakers from other countries who visit the factory and see the figures being made.

There are three ranges of porcelain figures – 'people', 'animals' and 'birds'. The expected monthly costs and sales information for each range is as follows:

Product	'People'	'Animals'	'Birds'
Sales and production units*	1,000	2,000	2,700
Labour hours per month	1,500	1,000	900
Total sales revenue	£60,000	£55,000	£47,250
Total direct materials	£5,000	£6,000	£5,400
Total direct labour	£15,000	£10,000	£9,000
Total variable overheads	£10,000	£9,000	£8,000

* note: a unit is a porcelain figure

The total expected monthly fixed costs relating to the production of all porcelain figures are £45,400.

Required:

(a) Complete the table below to show for each product range the expected contribution per unit.

Product	'People' £	'Animals' £	'Birds' £
Revenue per unit			
minus: Variable costs per unit			
Direct materials			
Direct labour			
Variable overheads per unit			
equals: Contribution per unit			

(b) If the company only produces the 'People' range, calculate the number of units it would need to make and sell each month to cover the fixed costs of £45,400.

(c) Making and painting the porcelain figures are highly skilled tasks, and unskilled labour cannot be brought in to cover for absent staff.

Unfortunately, because of staff illness, the available labour hours are reduced from 3,400 to 2,800. The finance director asks you to calculate the contribution of each unit (porcelain figure) per labour hour.

Using the data from (a), complete the table below.

Product	'People'	'Animals'	'Birds'
Contribution per unit			
Labour hours per unit			
Contribution per labour hour			

(d) Using the data from (c), calculate how many units of each of product ranges 'People', 'Animals' and 'Birds' the company should make and sell in order to maximise its profits using 2,800 labour hours.

....

....

....

....

....

....

....

....

....

....

....

....

....

....

9. You work as an Accounts Assistant at City News and Books, a company which owns a group of shops selling newspapers and magazines, books, and stationery. The accounting system has been set up to show the costs and revenue for each of the three sections of the business: newspapers and magazines, books, and stationery.

The following information has been extracted from the accounting system:

	Newspapers and magazines £000	Books £000	Stationery £000
Variable costs: materials	155	246	122
labour	65	93	58
Fixed costs*	80	125	45
Revenue	352	550	198
*apportioned to each section on the basis of revenue			

(a) The Finance Director knows that one of the sections is making a loss. She asks you to present the accounting information to show the costs and profit or loss for each section of the business.

(b) For the section of the business that is making a loss, the Finance Director asks you to give her a note of the points she should make to the directors of City News and Books regarding closure of that section.

10. The following information is available for the single product manufactured by a business.

Selling price per unit		£24.40
Variable costs per unit		£13.10
Fixed costs		£30,000
Budgeted production		5,000 units

    How many units must the business make and sell to produce a target profit of £20,000?

A	1,770 units	
B	2,655 units	
C	4,425 units	
D	5,000 units	

11. The accountant of Jadav Limited has produced the following budgeted income statement for the period April - June 20-6:

	£	£
Revenue (50,000 units at £5.00 each)		250,000
Variable costs	175,000	
Fixed costs	60,000	
		235,000
Profit for the period		15,000

    (a) What is the contribution sales ratio for Jadav Limited?

    (b) Calculate the number of units that must be made and sold for Jadav Limited to break-even.

    (c) If the directors of Jadav Limited require the company to achieve a profit of £45,000 for the period, how many units will need to be sold and at what total revenue?

Answers

Introduction to Financial Accounting	page 128
Financial Accounting	page 160
Management Accounting	page 184

INTRODUCTION TO FINANCIAL ACCOUNTING
ANSWERS

CHAPTERS 1-6: DOUBLE-ENTRY PROCEDURES; BUSINESS DOCUMENTS

1. (a) Two from:
    - To quantify items such as sales and expenses showing what transactions have happened in the past.
    - To record amounts due from trade receivables and due to trade payables and to take appropriate action.
    - To help reduce the risk of fraud by keeping detailed records which are maintained by several different individuals.
    - To enable the production of financial statements – income statement and statement of financial position.
    - To enable the production of forecasts for the future – forecast, or budgeted accounts – based on information from previous years.
    - To monitor performance by comparing actual outcomes with forecast outcomes, and to take appropriate action.
    - To provide information to the owner of the business and other stakeholders.

    (b) Three from:
    - bank: to ensure that borrowings are likely to be repaid
    - suppliers: to check the likelihood of receiving payment
    - customers: to check that the business can supply them with orders made
    - employees: to ensure that they will be paid their wages
    - trade unions: to ensure that employees are being offered the right terms and conditions
    - tax authorities: to ensure that tax due by the business on profits and for Value Added Tax has been paid
    - local community: to ensure that jobs are provided in the area
    - competitors: to compare the profitability of the business with their own
    - investors: to assess the return on their investment and the safety of their investment
    - potential investors: to assess the suitability of investing in the business

2. (a)

Transaction	Source document
Alcaria sold goods to Sam Brass for £275	Sales invoice
Sam Brass returned goods valued at £84 to Alcaria	Sales credit note
Sam Brass sent a cheque, after deducting a cash discount of £18, to Alcaria to clear the balance owing at 1 May	Bank paying-in slip counterfoil

(b)

Dr　　　　　　　　　　　　　　　　　　Sam Brass　　　　　　　　　　　　　　　　　　Cr

Date	Details	£	Date	Details	£
1 May	Balance b/d	745	16 May	Sales returns	84
7 May	Sales	275	24 May	Discount allowed	18
			24 May	Bank	727
			31 May	Balance c/d	191
		1,020			1,020
1 Jun	Balance b/d	191			

3. (a)

Item	Source document	Account to be debited	Account to be credited
1	Cheque counterfoil	Wages	Cash book/Bank
2	Purchases credit note	Trade payable/ Purchases ledger control account*	Purchases returns

* see chapter 11

(b)

Dr			Fashion Frocks			Cr
Date	Details	£	Date	Details		£
12 June	Bank	1,205	1 June	Balance b/d		1,275
12 June	Discount received	70	8 June	Purchases		950
18 June	Purchases returns	150	23 June	Purchases		650
30 June	Balance c/d	1,450				
		2,875				2,875
			1 July	Balance b/d		1,450

4. (a)

Transaction	Source document
Shoes from a manufacturer purchased on credit	Purchases invoice
Michel returned shoes to a manufacturer which had previously been purchased on credit	Purchases credit note
Cash and cheques deposited by Michel into the business bank account	Bank paying-in slip counterfoil
Michel paid a supplier by cheque	Cheque counterfoil
Michel sold 50 pairs of trainers to a sports centre. Payment will be made next month	Sales invoice

(b)

Transaction	Account to be debited	Account to be credited
A new shop till purchased from AJ Supplies on credit for £1,000	Shop equipment/fittings	AJ Supplies - trade payable
£5,000 paid into the business bank account from Michel's savings	Bank	Capital
Paid £1,200 to Shoe Traders, a supplier, in settlement of the account balance	Shoe Traders – trade payable	Bank
Paid shop rent of £750 by cheque	Rent	Bank

5.
- A business will extract a trial balance on a regular basis to check the arithmetic accuracy of the bookkeeping.
- However, a trial balance does not prove the complete accuracy of the accounting records – there are six types of errors that are not shown by the trial balance:
  1. Error of omission – a business transaction completely omitted from the accounting records
  2. Reversal of entries – debit and credit entries have been made in the accounts but on the wrong side of the two accounts concerned
  3. Mispost/error of commission – a transaction is entered to the wrong person's account
  4. Error of principle – a transaction is entered in the wrong type of account
  5. Error of original entry (or transcription) – the amount of a transaction is entered incorrectly in both accounts
  6. Compensating error – two errors cancel each other out
- A trial balance is also used as the starting point in the production of the financial statements of a business – income statement and statement of financial position.

6. A

7. C

8. D

9. (a)

Dr				Bank Account					Cr
Date 20-7	Details	Discount £	Bank £		Date 20-7	Details		Discount £	Bank £
26 Apr	Balance b/d		246		27 Apr	J Khan			332
27 Apr	A Monro		116		30 Apr	Raven Ltd		16	746
28 Apr	A Syed	10	425						
30 Apr	Balance c/d		291						
		10	1,078					16	1,078
					1 May	Balance b/d			291

GENERAL LEDGER

Dr			Discount Allowed			Cr
Date 20-7	Details		£	Date 20-7	Details	£
30 Apr	Bank		10			

Dr			Discount Received			Cr
Date 20-7	Details		£	Date 20-7	Details	£
				30 Apr	Bank	16

(b) **SALES LEDGER**

Dr			A Monro			Cr
Date 20-7	Details		£	Date 20-7	Details	£
6 Apr	Sales		316	27 Apr	Bank	116
				30 Apr	Balance c/d	200
			316			316
1 May	Balance b/d		200			

Dr			A Syed		Cr
Date 20-7	Details	£	Date 20-7	Details	£
8 Apr	Sales	435	28 Apr	Bank	425
			28 Apr	Discount allowed	10
		435			435

PURCHASES LEDGER

Dr			J Khan		Cr
Date 20-7	Details	£	Date 20-7	Details	£
27 Apr	Bank	332	1 Apr	Balance b/d	332
30 Apr	Balance c/d	454	11 Apr	Purchases	454
		786			786
			1 May	Balance b/d	454

Dr			Raven Ltd		Cr
Date 20-7	Details	£	Date 20-7	Details	£
30 Apr	Bank	746	13 Apr	Purchases	762
30 Apr	Discount received	16			
		762			762

10. (a)

BOOKS OF PRIME ENTRY

PURCHASES JOURNAL		
20-4		£
23 Jun	A Sanders	1,700
29 Jun	P Yarnton	1,056

PURCHASES RETURNS JOURNAL		
20-4		£
26 Jun	A Sanders	425

BANK ACCOUNT					
20-4		£	20-4		£
1 Jun	Balance b/d	1,027	25 Jun	T Smithers	418
			27 Jun	P Yarnton	147

(b)

PURCHASES (PAYABLES) LEDGER

A SANDERS ACCOUNT					
20-4		£	20-4		£
26 Jun	Purchases returns journal	425	23 Jun	Purchases journal	1,700

T SMITHERS ACCOUNT					
20-4		£	20-4		£
25 Jun	Bank	418	1 Jun	Balance b/d	440
25 Jun	Discount received	22			

P YARNTON ACCOUNT						
20-4			£	20-4		£
10 Jun	Purchases returns journal		130	1 Jun	Balance b/d	280
27 Jun	Bank		147	29 Jun	Purchases journal	1,056
27 Jun	Discount received		3			

(c)

DISCOUNT RECEIVED ACCOUNT						
20-4			£	20-4		£
				25 Jun	T Smithers	22
				27 Jun	P Yarnton	3

11. (a) The bookkeeper records day-to-day financial transactions, for example:
- maintaining accounting records
- entering transactions in the books of prime entry (journals) and ledger accounts
- checking the accuracy of the bookkeeping, including the extraction of a trial balance

(b) The accountant takes the financial information recorded by the bookkeeper, and uses it to:
- prepare and present financial reports to the business owners or managers, including the income statement and the statement of financial position
- apply accounting concepts to financial reports and statements
- ensure that financial reports and statements show a true and fair view of the business

CHAPTER 7: THE CASH BOOK

1. (i) Direct debit

Payments made by the bank from the account of their customer. It is the payee, or beneficiary, who originates the payment on the written instructions of the customer. Direct debits can be for fixed or variable amounts, and the payment dates can alter.

Electricity/gas bills and business rates are often paid by direct debit.

(ii) Standing order

Regular payments – eg monthly, weekly – made by the bank from the account of their customer. Payments are for fixed amounts, on the written instructions of the bank's customer.

Rent payments and loan repayments are often made by standing order.

2.

Cash Book

Dr											Cr
Date 20-7	Details	Discount £	Cash £	Bank £		Date 20-7	Details	Discount £	Cash £	Bank £	
3 Aug	Balance b/d		286			3 Aug	Balance b/d			3,472	
4 Aug	Sales		334			3 Aug	Rent			760	
5 Aug	Cash			500	C	5 Aug	Bank		500		C
5 Aug	Murphy Ltd	15		1,475		8 Aug	Rates			223	
10 Aug	Bank		400		C	8 Aug	JJ Supplies	10		490	
10 Aug	Balance c/d			3,370		10 Aug	Cash			400	C
						10 Aug	Wages		480		
						10 Aug	Balance c/d		40		
		15	1,020	5,345				10	1,020	5,345	
11 Aug	Balance b/d		40			11 Aug	Balance b/d			3,370	

3. (a) and (b)

Dr					Emma Maxwell Cash Book					Cr
Date 20-3	Details	Discount £	Cash £	Bank £	Date 20-3	Details		Discount £	Cash £	Bank £
1 Mar	Balance b/d		200		1 Mar	Balance b/d				1,898
6 Mar	Court Ltd			1,236	2 Mar	Lindum Supplies		6		254
13 Mar	H Sweeney	10		896	11 Mar	Rent				550
14 Mar	Sales		639		27 Mar	Wages			155	
28 Mar	Sales		786		20 Mar	Wyvern Council	SO			195
24 Mar	Mills & Co Ltd			477	21 Mar	Bank interest				45
31 Mar	Cash	C		1,270	31 Mar	Bank	C		1,270	
					31 Mar	Balances c/d			200	937
		10	1,625	3,879				6	1,625	3,879
1 Apr	Balances b/d		200	937						

(c)

Dr			Discount Allowed Account		Cr
Date 20-3	Details	£	Date 20-3	Details	£
31 Mar	Cash book	10			

Dr			Discount Received Account		Cr
Date 20-3	Details	£	Date 20-3	Details	£
			31 Mar	Cash book	6

CHAPTER 8: BANK RECONCILIATION STATEMENTS

1. (a) and (c) true; (b) and (d) false

2. It is important to reconcile the cash book to the **bank statement** on a **regular** basis.

The bank statement provides an **independent** accounting record and helps to prevent **fraud**.

It also highlights any **timing** differences and explains why there is a **discrepancy** between the bank statement balance and the **cash book** balance.

3. (a)

Dr   **Cash Book (bank columns)**   Cr

Details		£	Details		£
Balance b/d		743	Bank charges		25
Alportal Ltd		455	Wyvern Council		220
A Alta	adjustment	54	L Johnson		105
			A Alta	adjustment	45
			Balance c/d		857
		1,252			1,252
Balance b/d		857			

(b)   **Bank Reconciliation Statement at 27 April 20-1**

		£
Balance as per cash book		857
Add: unpresented cheque		
S Brass		126
		983
Less: amount not yet credited		
takings		275
Balance as per bank statement		708

(c) Three from:

- By comparing the transactions in the cash book and bank statement, any errors will be found and can be corrected (or advised to the bank, if the bank statement is wrong).
- The bank statement is an independent accounting record, therefore it will assist in deterring fraud by providing a means of verifying the cash book balance.
- By writing the cash book up-to-date, Jayne Carter's business has an amended figure for the bank balance to be shown in the trial balance.
- Unpresented cheques over six months old – out-of-date cheques – can be identified and written back in the cash book (any cheque dated more than six months ago will not be paid by the bank).
- It is good practice to prepare a bank reconciliation statement regularly so that any queries can be resolved.

answers - Chapter 8

4. (a)

Dr		Cash Book (bank columns)		Cr
Details	**£**	**Details**		**£**
Adjustment	645	Balance b/d		2,408
Balance c/d	2,837	A-Z Finance Ltd		485
		Bank interest and charges		124
		Adjustment		465
	3,482			3,482
		Balance b/d		2,837

(b)

Susana Villona

Bank Reconciliation Statement at 30 September 20-4

		£
Balance as per cash book		(2,837)
Add: unpresented cheque		
rent paid		750
		(2,087)
Less: amount not yet credited		
customer's cheque		368
Balance as per bank statement		(2,455)

(c)
- Her bank account is overdrawn and so the bank is a stakeholder in her business.
- The bank will wish to consider the profitability and liquidity of her business to ensure that the lending is safe.
- The bank will consider whether her business has the ability to meet the interest charged and to make repayment of the overdraft.
- The financial statements can assist the bank in deciding whether to allow the continuance of the overdraft facility.
- The bank may be able to give advice on the future financial management of her business.

5. (a) – (c)

CASH BOOK

Date	Details	Bank	Date	Cheque no	Details	Bank
20-8		£	20-8			£
1 Jun	Balance b/f	1,890	1 Jun	364125	Penryn Ltd	427
20 Jun	Chiverton Ltd	1,200	3 Jun	364126	Fal Boats	760
24 Jun	Perran Ltd	4,750	10 Jun	364127	S Mawes	4,200
24 Jun	P Porth	8,950	20 Jun	364128	Castle Supplies	1,062
23 Jun	Sand & Stone	2,486	20 Jun		J C Property Co	850
26 Jun	Surfrider Ltd	4,110	27 Jun		Vord Finance	275
			27 Jun		Balance c/d	15,812
		23,386				23,386
28 Jun	Balance b/d	15,812				

(d)

DURNING TRADING
Bank Reconciliation Statement as at 27 June 20-8

	£	£
Balance as per cash book		15,812
Add: unpresented cheque 364126 Fal Boats		760
		16,572
Less: amounts not yet credited		
Chiverton Ltd	1,200	
Perran Ltd	4,750	
P Porth	8,950	
		14,900
Balance as per bank statement		1,672

CHAPTER 9: INTRODUCTION TO FINANCIAL STATEMENTS

1.

Samantha Giardino
Income Statement
for the year ended 31 December 20-7

	£	£
Revenue		188,622
Opening inventory	21,945	
Purchases	110,233	
	132,178	
Less Closing inventory	18,762	
Cost of sales		113,416
Gross Profit		75,206
Less expenses:		
Salaries	37,390	
Heating and lighting	4,276	
Rent and business rates	6,849	
Sundry expenses	1,283	
Vehicle expenses	3,562	
		53,360
Profit for the year		21,846

Statement of Financial Position as at 31 December 20-7

	£	£	£
Non-current Assets			
Vehicles			20,450
Office equipment			10,960
			31,410
Current Assets			
Inventory		18,762	
Trade receivables		24,365	
		43,127	
Less Current Liabilities			
Trade payables	19,871		
Bank overdraft	2,454		
		22,325	
Net Current Assets or Working Capital			20,802
NET ASSETS			52,212
FINANCED BY			
Capital			
Opening capital			51,283
Add Profit for the year			21,846
			73,129
Less Drawings			20,917
			52,212

2. (a)

Alan Castle
Income Statement
for the year ended 30 June 20-3

	£	£
Gross Profit		55,430
Add discount received		210
		55,640
Less expenses:		
Salaries and wages	47,390	
Office expenses	2,750	
Vehicle expenses	6,840	
Bank charges	570	
		57,550
Loss for the year		1,910

(b)

Dr			**Capital Account**			Cr
20-3	Details	£	20-3	Details		£
30 Jun	Loss	1,910	30 Jun	Balance b/d		42,170
30 Jun	Drawings	8,460				
30 Jun	Balance c/d	31,800				
		42,170				42,170
			1 Jul	Balance b/d		31,800

3. **D**

4.

PQ Trading
Statement of Financial Position as at 30 September 20-2

	£	£	£
Non-current Assets			
Property			175,000
Office equipment			16,450
			191,450
Current Assets			
Inventory		16,345	
Trade receivables		24,540	
Cash		496	
		41,381	
Less Current Liabilities			
Trade payables	21,364		
Bank overdraft	5,145	26,509	
Net Current Assets or Working Capital			14,872
			206,322
Less Non-current Liabilities			
Mortgage on business premises			100,000
NET ASSETS			106,322
FINANCED BY			
Capital		W1	102,772
Add Profit for the year			24,550
Less Drawings			21,000
			106,322

W1 Capital   106,322 + 21,000 − 24,550 = 102,772

CHAPTER 10: THE GENERAL JOURNAL AND CORRECTION OF ERRORS

1.

Error in the general ledger	Error disclosed by the trial balance	Error not disclosed by the trial balance
A bank payment for telephone expenses has been recorded on the debit side of both the cash book and telephone expenses account	✔	
A payment recorded in bank account for vehicle repairs has been entered in vehicles account		✔
A sales invoice has been omitted from all accounting records		✔
The balance of purchases returns account has been calculated incorrectly	✔	
A bank payment of £85 for stationery has been recorded as £58 in both accounts		✔

2. D

3. D

4.

Dr	Suspense Account			Cr
Details	£	Details		£
Opening balance	21	Purchases returns		345
Purchases returns	354	Purchases		100
Discount received	70			
	445			445

5. (a)

Dr	Suspense Account			Cr
Details	£	Details		£
Discount allowed	100	Opening balance	W1	1,158
Vehicle expenses	86	Vehicle expenses		68
Discount received	40			
Rent paid	500			
Rent income	500			
	1,226			1,226

W1 Opening balance (trial balance difference) 364,859 – 363,701 = 1,158

(b)

Error	Increase profit £	Reduce profit £	No effect on profit (✓)
(1)	100		
(2)	18		
(3)	40		
(4)		175	
(5)	1,000		

CHAPTER 11: CONTROL ACCOUNTS

1. **B**

2.

Purchases Ledger Control Account

Date 20-3	Details	Amount £	Date 20-3	Details	Amount £
31 May	Bank	13,750	1 May	Balance b/d	50,300
31 May	Discount received	500	31 May	Purchases	21,587
31 May	Purchases returns	250			
31 May	Balance c/d	57,387			
		71,887			71,887
			1 Jun	Balance b/d	57,387

3. (a)

Dr   **Purchases Ledger Control Account**   **Cr**

Date 20-1	Details	£	Date 20-1	Details	£
30 April	Bank	37,396	1 April	Balance b/d	33,154
30 April	Purchases returns	1,532	30 April	Purchases	42,805
30 April	Discount received	741	30 April	Bank	842
30 April	Contra: sales ledger	585			
30 April	Balance c/d	36,547			
		76,801			76,801
			1 May	Balance b/d	36,547

(b)
- The balance of purchases ledger control account should agree with the total of the individual account balances in purchases ledger.
- If these do not agree there will be errors in the purchases ledger, in the purchases ledger control account, or in both.

(c) One from:
- Some types of errors (mispost/error of commission, compensating error, error of omission, error of original entry) will not be revealed by purchases ledger control account; thus the ledger accounts will be thought to be correct when they are not.
- Purchases ledger control account may indicate that there is an error within the ledger section, but will not pinpoint where the error has occurred.

4. (a)

Dr				Sales Ledger Control Account		Cr
Date 20-1	Details	£	Date 20-1	Details		£
1 June	Balance b/d	45,027	30 June	Sales returns		1,475
30 June	Sales	61,322	30 June	Bank		55,396
30 June	Bank	345	30 June	Discount allowed		1,027
			30 June	Contra: purchases ledger		824
			30 June	Balance c/d		47,972
		106,694				106,694
1 July	Balance b/d	47,972				

(b)
- The balance of her sales ledger control account should agree with the total of the individual account balances in sales ledger.
- If these do not agree there will be errors in the sales ledger, in the sales ledger control account, or in both.

(c) Two from:
- Mispost/error of commission – where a transaction is entered in the wrong person's account (eg J Smith instead of J Smithson).
- Compensating error – where two errors cancel each other out (eg an overcast of £100 on one sales ledger account is cancelled out by an undercast on another sales ledger account).
- Error of omission – where a business transaction has been completely omitted from the accounting records.
- Error of original entry (or transcription) – the amount of a transaction is entered incorrectly in both accounts (eg an amount for £54 is entered as £45).

5. (a)

Sales Ledger Control Account

Dr					Cr
Date 20-2	Details	£	Date 20-2	Details	£
31 Aug	Balance b/d	18,870	31 Aug	Balance adjustment W1	90
31 Aug	Sales	1,000	31 Aug	Discount allowed	125
31 Aug	Bank (dishonoured cheque)	395	31 Aug	Irrecoverable debt	220
			31 Aug	Purchases ledger (contra)	175
			31 Aug	Balance c/d	19,655
		20,265			20,265
1 Sep	Balance b/d	19,655			

W1 Balance adjustment   18,870 − 18,780 = 90

(b) Three from:

- Verifies the arithmetical accuracy of the total of the sales ledger accounts.
- Provides managers with a total figure for trade receivables.
- Provides a figure for trade receivables for the trial balance and statement of financial position.
- Helps in the prevention of fraud.
- Helps in the location of errors within individual sales ledger accounts.

CHAPTER 12: ADJUSTMENTS TO FINANCIAL STATEMENTS

1. (a) Accrued expenses

    Accrued expenses are amounts due in an accounting period which are unpaid at the end of that period.

    In financial statements accrued expenses are:

    - added to the expense in the trial balance before listing it in the income statement – in this way, profit for the year will be reduced
    - shown as a current liability (other payables) in the year-end statement of financial position

   (b) Prepaid expenses

    Prepaid expenses are payments made in advance of the accounting period to which they relate.

    In financial statements prepaid expenses are:

    - deducted from the expenses in the trial balance before listing it in the income statement – in this way, profit for the year will be increased
    - shown as a current asset (other receivables) in the year-end statement of financial position

2. A

3.

Shelley Smith
Income Statement for the year ended 31 December 20-3

		£	£
Revenue			124,380
Sales returns			(490)
Net Revenue			123,890
Opening inventory		27,170	
Purchases		85,210	
Carriage inwards		1,340	
Purchases returns		(1,520)	
		112,200	
Closing inventory		(29,210)	
Cost of sales			82,990
Gross profit			40,900
Add: Discount received			970
			41,870
Less Expenses:			
Discount allowed		460	
General expenses		16,450	
Depreciation of shop fittings	W1	1,500	
Rent and business rates	W2	10,080	
Telephone expenses		1,260	
			29,750
Profit for the year			12,120

W1	Depreciation of shop fittings	8,300 − 800 = 7,500 ÷ 5 = 1,500
W2	Rent and business rates	10,160 + 250 − 330 (1,320 ÷ 12 × 3 months) = 10,080

answers - Chapter 12

4. (a)

Richard Farley:
Income Statement for the year ended 31 March 20-3

		£	£
Revenue			154,360
Sales returns			(430)
Net revenue			153,930
Opening inventory		24,830	
Purchases		76,250	
Carriage inwards		850	
		101,930	
Closing inventory		(26,450)	
Cost of sales			75,480
Gross profit			78,450
Add: Discount received			790
			79,240
Less Expenses:			
Discount allowed		180	
General expenses		11,470	
Heating and lighting		2,720	
Rent and business rates	W1	13,210	
Wages and salaries	W2	38,090	
Depreciation of shop fittings	W3	2,680	
Irrecoverable debt written off		240	
			68,590
Profit for the year			10,650

W1	Rent and business rates	18,390 − 5,180 = 13,210
W2	Wages and salaries	37,260 + 830 = 38,090
W3	Depreciation of shop fittings	(15,200 − 1,800) ÷ 5 = 2,680

(b)

Richard Farley: Statement of Financial Position as at 31 March 20-3

		£	£
Non-current Assets			
Shop fittings at cost		15,200	
Less depreciation	W1	8,040	
Net book value			7,160
Current Assets			
Inventory		26,450	
Trade receivables	W2	3,300	
Other receivables	W3	5,180	
		34,930	
Less Current Liabilities			
Bank overdraft	W4	80	
Trade payables		6,220	
Other payables		830	
		7,130	
Net Current Assets or Working Capital			27,800
			34,960
Less Non-current Liabilities			
Bank loan (repayable September 20-8)			(7,600)
NET ASSETS			27,360
FINANCED BY			
Capital at 1 April 20-2			29,250
Increase in capital			2,500
Add Profit for the year			10,650
			42,400
Less Drawings			15,040
			27,360

W1	Depreciation of shop fittings	5,360 + 2,680 = 8,040
W2	Trade receivables	3,540 – 240 = 3,300
W3	Prepaid expense	10,360 ÷ 2 = 5,180
W4	Bank overdraft	2,580 – 2,500 = 80

5.

Susie Leah: Statement of Financial Position as at 31 December 20-6

		£000	£000
Non-current Assets			
Property at cost			220
Office equipment at cost		60	
Less depreciation		35	
Net book value			25
			245
Current Assets			
Inventory		18	
Trade receivables	W1	12	
Other receivables		3	
		33	
Less Current Liabilities			
Trade payables		18	
Other payables	W2	5	
Bank overdraft	W3	4	
		27	
Net Current Assets or Working Capital			6
			251
Less Non-current Liabilities			
Mortgage on premises (repayable 20-9)			(150)
NET ASSETS			101
FINANCED BY			
Capital at 1 January 20-6			103
Add Profit for the year	W4		18
			121
Less Drawings			20
			101

W1	Trade receivables	15 – 2 – 1 = 12
W2	Accrued expenses	2 + 3 = 5
W3	Bank overdraft	6 – 2 = 4
W4	Profit for the year	22 – 3 – 1 = 18

6. (a)

	Effect on profit £	£
Profit for the year		**25,000**
1. Wages owing	(1,480)	
2. Rent paid in advance	1,100	
3. Vehicle depreciation	(7,700)	
4. Inventory understated	2,000	
5. Loan repayment	no effect	
6. Direct bank transfer received from trade receivable	no effect	
7. Irrecoverable debt written off	(250)	
Adjusted profit for the year		18,670

(b)

Lydia Duarte: Statement of Financial Position as at 30 September 20-5

		£	£
Non-current Assets			
Vehicles at cost		38,500	
Less depreciation	W1	23,100	
Net book value			15,400
Current Assets			
Inventory	W2	38,430	
Trade receivables	W3	23,260	
Other receivables	W4	1,830	
		63,520	
Less Current Liabilities			
Bank overdraft	W5	2,350	
Loan	W6	11,000	
Trade payables		16,150	
Other payables	W7	2,070	
		31,570	
Net Current Assets or Working Capital			31,950
NET ASSETS			47,350

FINANCED BY

Capital at 1 October 20-4	42,440
Add Profit for the year	18,670
	61,110
Less Drawings	13,760
	47,350

W1	Depreciation of vehicles	15,400 + 7,700 = 23,100
W2	Inventories	36,430 + 2,000 = 38,430
W3	Trade receivables	24,310 − 800 − 250 = 23,260
W4	Prepaid expenses	730 + 1,100 = 1,830
W5	Bank overdraft	2,150 + 1,000 − 800 = 2,350
W6	Loan	12,000 − 1,000 = 11,000
W7	Accrued expenses	590 + 1,480 = 2,070

7. (a) (i)

	£
vehicles at cost	74,000
less depreciation to 1 January 20-3	33,500
net book value at 1 January 20-3	40,500
depreciation charge for year = 40,500 x 30%	12,150

(ii)

	£
machinery at cost	37,000
depreciation charge for year = 37,000 x 20%	7,400

(b)

KAREN
Statement of Financial Position (extract) as at 31 December 20-3

Non-current Assets		£	£
Vehicles at cost		74,000	
Less depreciation	W1	45,650	
Net book value			28,350
Machinery at cost		37,000	
Less depreciation	W2	19,650	
Net book value			17,350
			45,700

W1 Vehicles – provision for depreciation: 33,500 + 12,150 = 45,650
W2 Machinery – provision for depreciation: 12,250 + 7,400 = 19,650

8. (a) **Private expenses**

Private expenses are where the owner uses business facilities for private purposes – eg telephone or car. The owner will agree the amount that is to be charged to him/her as drawings, while the other part represents a business expense.

In the double-entry accounts, the expense account is credited and the owner's drawings amount is debited with the private amount. The remaining balance of the expense account is then charged to the income statement, after adjustment for any accruals or prepayments. The balance of drawings account is shown on the statement of financial position as a deduction from capital and, in the double-entry accounts, is debited to the owner's capital account.

(b) **Goods for owner's use**

When the owner of a business takes some of the goods in which the business trades for his/her own use, the amount is:
– debited to the owner's drawings account
– credited to purchases account

The reason for crediting purchases account is to reduce the amount of purchases and record only those purchases used in the business, which are then matched with the sales derived from them.

(c) **Goods on sale or return sent to a customer**

Sale or return is where a business supplies goods to a customer on the basis that the customer will pay for the goods as and when they are sold. Until the goods are paid for by the customer they remain the property of the supplier and are included in the supplier's inventory. If the goods are not sold within an agreed time period, the goods will be returned to the supplier. Usually the invoice issued for such goods will be marked clearly as 'sale or return'.

Accounting entries in the supplier's accounting records include:

- supply of goods on sale or return to a customer
    - debit trade receivable's account
    - credit sales account
- payment received for some or all of the goods
    - debit bank account
    - credit trade receivable's account

At the supplier's financial year-end, any unsold goods on sale or return are included in inventory, at the cost to the supplier and sales revenue is reduced by the unsold amount.

FINANCIAL ACCOUNTING
ANSWERS

CHAPTER 13: BUSINESS ORGANISATIONS AND FINANCING

1. *Advantages*

   Two from:

   - Limited liability – if the business fails then Erica will lose only the amount of her investment in the company and, unlike a sole trader or a partnership, her personal assets cannot be taken to pay the debts of the company.

   - Separate legal entity – anyone taking legal action proceeds against the company and not the individual shareholder(s); also, a limited company does not finish when the owner retires or dies – it can be sold on to others.

   - Decision-making – as Erica will be the only shareholder she can continue to take all the decisions; in larger companies this will not be the case.

   - Raising finance – Erica may be able to raise finance more easily from relatives and friends, and from venture capital companies; raising bank loans is usually easier for a company than for a sole trader or partnership.

   - Other factors – a limited company often has a higher status and standing in the business community, and this may allow for expansion in the future.

   Disadvantages

   Two from:

   - Legal and accountancy costs – setting up a private limited company has start-up costs and annual costs will be higher than for a sole trader or partnership.

   - Legal requirements – the administration of a company is greater than for a sole trader/partnership as the company must be registered at Companies House, formal annual financial statements must be produced and filed at Companies House, and the annual financial statements may need to be audited (depending on the size of the business).

   - Published financial statements – Erica must ensure that her accounting records are of a sufficient standard to enable annual financial statements to be completed (her accountant will charge more for preparing the financial statements of a limited company than for a sole trader or partnership), and her annual financial statements will be available through Companies House for anyone to see.

answers - Chapter 13

2. Two from:

- **Legal requirements**

    Setting up a private limited company is more complex and start-up costs will be higher than for a sole trader or partnership:
    - the company must be registered at Companies House
    - formal annual financial statements must be prepared and filed at Companies House
    - the annual financial statements may have to be audited, depending on the size of the business

- **Control of the company**

    Jane and Scott's business requires capital of £70,000 but their contribution will be £15,000 each. This means that £40,000 will have to be raised from selling shares or from other forms of finance. If a shareholder buys more than half of all shares in issue, then Jane and Scott will lose control of their business and will not be able to run it as they wish.

- **Dividend payments**

    Outside shareholders will be looking to invest in Jane and Scott's company with a view to receiving income in the form of dividends. This means that Jane and Scott must share the profits with others instead of between themselves.

- **Conclusion**

    Whilst it is far simpler for Jane and Scott to form a partnership, they must weigh up whether or not the disadvantages of forming a company are outweighed by the benefits of limited liability which a company will give.

3.

	Ann	Bee	Cat
Ratio of 1 : 1 : 1	£40,000	£40,000	£40,000
Ratio of 1 : 2 : 1	£30,000	£60,000	£30,000
Ratio of 2 : 2 : 1	£48,000	£48,000	£24,000

4. (a) Purchase of the next door premises
- the accountant proposes borrowing £700,000, being 70% of the cost – the maximum that most lenders would be prepared to finance
- the interest cost per year will be £35,000
- the 15-year term suggested by the accountant is very reasonable as the term could be up to 25 years
- an arrangement fee will be charged by the lender
- security will be required by the lender, usually the property being financed

- repayments on the commercial mortgage – capital and interest – will have to be made for fifteen years, usually on a monthly basis (which makes for easy budgeting)
- the other part of the cost of the new premises, £300,000, needs to be financed, possibly through a share issue or directors' loans. Do the four directors have private funds for this, or are there new shareholders that will contribute?
- if new shares are issued to other parties, the directors' holdings will be diluted as they will no longer own the whole company
- are there likely to be sufficient future profits to pay dividends?
- the benefit of using shares to fund part of the purchase cost is that repayments do not need to be made to shareholders
- debentures – loan notes – are another source of finance, subject to finding a lender; the disadvantage of debentures, from the company's viewpoint, is that interest must always be paid on time even if losses are made

(b) Funding the refurbishment and alteration costs

Bank overdraft:
- a suitable financing method for funding the short-term requirements of an expanding business
- if whole £40,000 overdraft used for full twelve months, interest will be £2,800 (£40,000 x 7%)
- the actual interest charge may well be lower as it is calculated on a daily basis on the actual amount overdrawn
- security will be required by the bank to safeguard the borrowing
- interest rates can be higher than bank loan rates
- an overdraft is repayable on demand if the bank wants the borrowing repaid

Bank short-term loan:
- a twelve-month loan can be arranged to provide the required finance
- usually loan repayments are made on a monthly basis, but it may be possible to arrange a 'repayment holiday' to delay early repayments
- if whole £40,000 loan used for full twelve months, interest would be £2,400 (£40,000 x 6%)
- security will be required by the bank to safeguard the borrowing

Other considerations:
- will £40,000 be sufficient?
- the budgeted financial statements could prove to be incorrect
- arrangement fees will be charged by the bank for both forms of borrowing
- on the face of it, the bank short-term loan is cheaper than an overdraft but will depend on how much of the overdraft facility is used
- can the refurbishment and alterations be completed to the cost estimates and timescales?
- will bookings for the refurbished rooms be at a sufficient level to meet the budgeted figures?

CHAPTER 14: ACCOUNTING CONCEPTS AND INVENTORY VALUATION

1. (a) (i) **Prudence**

    This concept requires that caution is exercised when making judgements under conditions of uncertainty. This means that, where there is any doubt, a conservative (lower) figure for profit and the valuation of assets should be reported. To this end, profits are not to be anticipated and should only be recognised when it is reasonably certain that they will be actually made; at the same time, all known liabilities should be provided for.

    (ii) **Consistency**

    This concept requires that, when a business adopts particular accounting policies, it should continue to use such policies consistently. For example, a business that decides to make a provision for depreciation at ten per cent per year, using the straight-line method, should continue to use that method for future financial statements for this asset. However, having chosen a particular policy, a business is entitled to make changes provided there are good reasons for so doing, and a note to the financial statements would explain what has happened.

   (b) The application of the prudence concept to the preparation of the financial statements of a business prevents an over-optimistic presentation of the assets, liabilities and profit.

    Examples of the use of the prudence concept include:

    - accrual of expenses and income, where an estimate is made of the amount
    - prepayment of expenses and income, where an estimate is made of the amount
    - inventory valuation – at the lower of cost and net realisable value
    - depreciation of non-current assets
    - irrecoverable debts written off
    - provision for doubtful debts

    The application of the consistency concept ensures that a direct comparison between the financial statements of different years can be made. The use of ratio analysis to interpret the financial statements of a business over two or more years is meaningful where the consistency concept has been applied.

    Examples of the use of the consistency concept include:

    - inventory valuation
    - depreciation of non-current assets
    - provision for doubtful debts
    - the application of the materiality concept (which establishes which items are of sufficient value to be recorded separately in the financial statements)

2. B

3. (a)

Cost	100 x £15	=	£1,500
Net realisable value	100 x £17.50	=	£1,750
Less advertising costs			£300
			£1,450

Applying the rule of 'lower of cost and net realisable value', the inventory should be valued at £1,450 for the financial statements for the year ended 31 December 20-4.

(b) Prudence

4. B

5.

Item	Effect on profit	Concept
(1) Fee for audit and tax advice	(7,500)	Accruals
(2) Rent	1,500	Accruals
(3) Depreciation	(7,000)	Consistency/Prudence
(4) Inventory	(200)	Consistency/Prudence
(5) Irrecoverable debt	(2,000)	Prudence/Realisation

Tutorial note: the assumption is that the business is a going concern and that all amounts are considered to be material.

CHAPTER 15: FURTHER ASPECTS OF FINANCIAL STATEMENTS

1. B

2. D

3. C

4. (a) 21,040 x 3% = £631.20

   (b)
	£
Closing provision	631.20
Opening provision	550.80
Increase in provision	80.40

   Therefore profit for the year ended 31 October 20-8 will be reduced by £80.40.

   (c)
	£
Trade receivables	21,040.00
Less provision for doubtful debts	631.20
Net trade receivables to be shown in the SoFP	20,408.80

5.

Dr	Computer Disposal Account			Cr
		£		£
Computer W1		3,500	Provision for depreciation	2,500
			Bank (disposal proceeds)	350
			Income statement (loss on sale)	650
		3,500		3,500

W1 Cost of computer: £1,000 + £2,500

6. (a)

		£
	Cost	12,000
Less	Depreciation	5,250
Equals	Net book value	6,750
	Sale proceeds	6,500
Equals	Loss on sale	250

(b)

	£
Cost: 46,000 – disposals 12,000 + addition 16,250 =	50,250
Depreciation: 22,000 – 5,250 =	16,750
	33,500

Depreciation charge for year = 33,500 x 25% = 8,375

7.

GENERAL LEDGER

Dr **Inventory Account** Cr

20-8			£	20-8			£
Jan	1	Balance b/d	12,240	Dec	31	Income statement	12,240
Dec	31	Income statement	14,050	Dec	31	Balance c/d	14,050
			26,290				26,290
20-9				20-9			
Jan	1	Balance b/d	14,050				

Dr **Provision for Depreciation (Vehicles) Account** Cr

20-8			£	20-8			£
Dec	31	Balance c/d	19,520	Jan	1	Balance b/d	14,400
				Dec	31	Income statement (W1)	5,120
			19,520				19,520
20-9				20-9			
				Jan	1	Balance b/d	19,520

Provision for Doubtful Debts Account

Dr 20-8			£	20-8			£
Dec	31	Income statement (W2)	64	Jan	1	Balance b/d	720
Dec	31	Balance c/d	656				
			720				720
20-9				20-9			
				Jan	1	Balance b/d	656

Rent Income Account

Dr 20-8			£	20-8			£
Jan	1	Balance b/d	220	Jan-Dec		Bank	4,180
Dec	31	Income statement	4,500	Dec	31	Balance c/d	540
			4,720				4,720
20-9				20-9			
Jan	1	Balance b/d	540				

Vehicle Expenses Account

Dr 20-8			£	20-8			£
Jan-Dec		Bank	3,230	Jan	1	Balance b/d	170
				Dec	31	Income statement	2,810
				Dec	31	Balance c/d	250
			3,230				3,230
20-9				20-9			
Jan	1	Balance b/d	250				

W1 Provision for depreciation: 20% x (£40,000 − £14,400) = £5,120
W2 Provision for doubtful debts: £720 − (£16,400 x 4%) = £64 decrease

8.

ALEX MUNRO
Income Statement for the year ended 30 April 20-3

		£	£
Fee income			86,245
Add income:			
Recovery of irrecoverable debts			195
Rent income	W1		1,820
Decrease in provision for doubtful debts	W2		150
			88,410
Less expenses:			
Salaries		33,470	
Irrecoverable debts		255	
Administration expenses		24,075	
Discount allowed		315	
Depreciation of non-current assets	W3	10,000	
Loss on sale of vehicle	W4	750	
			68,865
Profit for the year			19,545

W1 Rent income = 2,360 − 540 paid in advance = 1,820

W2 Provision for doubtful debts = 460 − 310 = 150 reduction in provision

W3 £25,000 provision for depreciation at start of year − £7,500 depreciation on vehicle sold = £17,500. £27,500 provision for depreciation at end of year − £17,500 = £10,000 depreciation for year (as shown in income statement)

W4

	£
Net book value (£12,000 − £7,500)	4,500
Sale price	3,750
Loss on sale	750

9.

TAMSIN SMITH

Income Statement for the year ended 30 June 20-4

		£	£
Gross profit	W1		14,190
Add income:			
Rent income	W2	4,950	
Recovery of irrecoverable debts		220	
Decrease in provision for doubtful debts	W3	52	
			5,222
			19,412
Less expenses:			
Operating expenses	W4	6,735	
Depreciation: vehicles	W5	4,500	
Depreciation: shop fittings	W6	3,400	
Irrecoverable debts		590	
			15,225
Profit for the year			4,187

W1   Gross profit = 14,760 – 570 reduction in closing inventory = 14,190

W2   Rent income = 5,600 – 650 paid in advance = 4,950

W3   Provision for doubtful debts = 8,310 – 590 = 7,720 x 2.5% = 193 – 245 = 52 decrease in provision

W4   Operating expenses = 6,240 + 495 = 6,735

W5   Provision for depreciation: vehicles = 32,000 – 14,000 = 18,000 x 25% = 4,500

W6   Provision for depreciation: shop fittings = 17,000 x 20% = 3,400

CHAPTER 16: PREPARING SOLE TRADER FINANCIAL STATEMENTS

1.

ANTON BUSZCZAK
Income Statement for the year ended 30 June 20-6

		£	£
Revenue			145,630
Opening inventory		4,525	
Purchases		59,450	
		63,975	
Less Closing inventory		5,385	
Cost of sales			58,590
Gross profit			87,040
Less expenses:			
Vehicle running expenses	W1	3,790	
Rent and business rates		12,080	
Office expenses	W2	6,680	
Discount allowed		580	
Wages and salaries		43,190	
Depreciation: machinery		4,000	
vehicles		8,500	
			78,820
Profit for the year			8,220

Statement of Financial Position as at 30 June 20-6

	£	£	£
Non-current Assets	Cost	Depreciation	Net book value
Machinery	25,000	W3 15,000	10,000
Vehicles	33,000	W4 20,700	12,300
	58,000	35,700	22,300
Current Assets			
Inventory		5,385	
Trade receivables		4,155	
Other receivables		175	
Bank		3,365	
		13,080	
Less Current Liabilities			
Trade payables	10,845		
Other payables	345		
		11,190	
Net Current Assets or Working Capital			1,890
NET ASSETS			24,190
FINANCED BY			
Capital			
Opening capital			28,550
Add Profit for the year			8,220
			36,770
Less Drawings			12,580
			24,190

W1   Vehicle running expenses = 3,965 – 175 = 3,790
W2   Office expenses = 6,335 + 345 = 6,680
W3   Provision for depreciation: machinery = 11,000 + 4,000 = 15,000
W4   Provision for depreciation: vehicles = 12,200 + 8,500 = 20,700

2. (a) **SAMANTHA MARTINEZ**
Income Statement for the year ended 30 September 20-4

		£	£
Revenue			245,084
Opening inventory		5,893	
Purchases (less £750 goods for own use)		155,277	
		161,170	
Less Closing inventory		7,541	
Cost of sales			153,629
Gross profit			91,455
Add income:			
Recovery of irrecoverable debts			176
Decrease in provision for doubtful debts	W1		93
			91,724
Less expenses:			
Office salaries	W2	50,643	
Business rates and insurance	W3	6,201	
Administration expenses		17,122	
Irrecoverable debts		295	
Depreciation: property	W4	4,400	
office equipment	W5	7,125	
			85,786
Profit for the year			5,938

W1   Provision for doubtful debts = 18,400 trade receivables x 3% provision = 552 – 645 = £93 decrease in provision

W2   Office salaries = 50,133 + 510 = 50,643

W3   Business rates and insurance = 6,433 – 232 = 6,201

W4   Provision for depreciation: property = 220,000 x 2% = 4,400

W5   Provision for depreciation: office equipment = 45,000 – 16,500 = 28,500 x 25% = 7,125

(b) **Capital**

	£
Opening capital	160,500
Add Profit for the year	5,938
	166,438
Less Drawings (plus £750 goods for own use)	22,900
	143,538

3.

CHARLOTTE LEE
Income Statement for the year ended 31 December 20-5

		£	£
Gross profit	W1		67,606
Add income:			
Rent income	W2		7,244
Profit on sale of vehicle	W3		270
			75,120
Less expenses:			
Irrecoverable debts		245	
Operating expenses	W4	25,354	
Wages	W5	40,687	
Depreciation: vehicle	W6	1,920	
fixtures and fittings	W7	4,960	
Increase in provision for doubtful debts	W8	158	
			73,324
Profit for the year			1,796

W1   Gross profit = 67,386 – 400 inventory reduction + 620 drawings = 67,606

W2   Rent income = 7,864 – 620 paid in advance = 7,244

W3   Profit on sale of vehicle = 15,000 – 5,400 = 9,600 x 20% = 1,920 depreciation for year = 7,680 net book value. 7,950 disposal proceeds – 7,680 net book value = 270 profit on sale

W4   Operating expenses = 32,149 – 295 paid in advance – 6,500 purchase of fixtures = 25,354

W5   Wages = 40,231 + 456 owing = 40,687

W6   Provision for depreciation: vehicle = 15,000 – 5,400 = 9,600 x 20% = 1,920

W7   Provision for depreciation: fixtures and fittings = 18,300 + 6,500 = 24,800 x 20% = 4,960

W8   Provision for doubtful debts = 24,200 trade receivables x 4% provision = 968 – 810 = £158 increase in provision

4.

HENRY DUNSTONE
Income Statement for the year ended 31 March 20-7

		£	£
Revenue			283,135
Less Returns			1,068
Net Revenue			282,067
Opening inventory		33,940	
Purchases	W1	134,765	
		168,705	
Less Closing inventory		36,875	
Cost of sales			131,830
Gross profit			150,237
Add income:			
Discount received			741
			150,978
Less expenses:			
Discount allowed		862	
Operating expenses		35,336	
Rent and business rates	W2	16,072	
Salaries	W3	94,550	
Increase in provision for doubtful debts	W4	386	
Depreciation: fixtures and fittings	W5	4,560	
machinery	W6	7,104	
			158,870
Loss for the year			7,892

Statement of Financial Position as at 31 March 20-7

	£	£	£
Non-current Assets	Cost	Depreciation	Net book value
Fixtures and fittings	30,400	13,680	16,720
Machinery	55,500	27,084	28,416
	85,900	40,764	45,136
Current Assets			
Inventory		36,875	
Trade receivables W7		55,809	
Other receivables		1,950	
		94,634	
Less Current Liabilities			
Trade payables	49,833		
Other payables	1,465		
Bank	4,107		
		55,405	
Net Current Assets or Working Capital			39,229
NET ASSETS			84,365
FINANCED BY			
Capital			103,856
Less Loss for the year			7,892
			95,964
Less Drawings W8			11,599
			84,365

W1 Purchases = 136,240 – 1,475 goods for own use = 134,765
W2 Rent and business rates = 18,022 – 1,950 = 16,072
W3 Salaries = 93,085 + 1,465 = 94,550
W4 Provision for doubtful debts = 57,240 x 2.5% = 1,431 – 1,045 = 386 increase in provision
W5 Provision for depreciation: fixtures and fittings = 30,400 x 15% = 4,560
W6 Provision for depreciation: machinery = 55,500 – 19,980 = 35,520 x 20% = 7,104
W7 Trade receivables = 57,240 – 1,431 provision for doubtful debts = 55,809
W8 Drawings = 10,124 + 1,475 goods for own use = 11,599

CHAPTER 17: FINANCIAL STATEMENTS OF LIMITED COMPANIES

1. D

2.

Item	Heading
Tax liabilities	Current liabilities
Share premium	Capital reserve
Buildings	Non-current assets
Retained earnings	Revenue reserve
Ordinary shares	Issued share capital
Debentures (repayable in five years' time)	Non-current liabilities

3.

Axiom plc

Statement of Changes in Equity for the year ended 30 June 20-5

	Issued share capital £	Share premium £	Retained earnings £	Total £
At 1 July 20-4	600,000	90,000	330,000	1,020,000
Issue of shares	150,000	90,000		240,000
Profit for the year			365,000	365,000
Dividends paid			(220,000)	(220,000)
At 30 June 20-5	750,000	180,000	475,000	1,405,000

answers - Chapter 17

4.

Bohan Ltd

Statement of Changes in Equity for the year ended 31 December 20-2

	Issued share capital £	Share premium £	Retained earnings £	Total £
At 1 January 20-2	220,000	–	118,000	338,000
Issue of shares	110,000	66,000		176,000
Profit for the year			79,000	79,000
Dividends paid			(45,000)	(45,000)
At 31 December 20-2	330,000	66,000	152,000	548,000

5. (a) **Definition:** Capital reserves are created as a result of a non-trading profit – they cannot be used to fund dividend payments.

Example: Share premium account.

(b) **Definition:** Revenue reserves are profits from trading activities which have been retained in the company to help build the company for the future.

Example: Retained earnings.

6. (a)

AKRAM LTD
Income Statement for the year ended 31 December 20-4

		£	£
Gross profit			148,800
Expenses:			
Operating expenses		92,530	
Depreciation	W1	25,200	
			(117,730)
Profit for the year from operations			31,070
Finance costs	W2		(1,800)
Profit for the year before tax			29,270
Tax	W3		(5,854)
Profit for the year after tax			23,416

W1 Depreciation: (£120,000 – £36,000) x 30%
W2 Finance costs: £30,000 x 6%
W3 Tax: £29,270 x 20%

(b)

AKRAM LTD
Statement of Changes In Equity for the year ended 31 December 20-4

	Issued share capital £	Share premium £	Retained earnings £	Total £
Balances at start	100,000	10,000	35,471	145,471
Profit for the year			23,416	23,416
Dividends paid			(20,000)	(20,000)
Issue of shares	25,000	20,000		45,000
Balances at end	125,000	30,000	38,887	193,887

(c)

AKRAM LTD

Statement of Financial Position as at 31 December 20-4

	£ Cost	£ Depreciation	£ Carrying amount
Non-current Assets			
Non-current assets	120,000	(W1) 61,200	58,800
Current Assets			
Inventory		25,364	
Trade receivables		38,196	
Cash and cash equivalents		135,427	
		198,987	
Less Current Liabilities			
Trade payables	27,146		
Other payables	(W2) 6,754		
		(33,900)	
Net Current Assets			165,087
			223,887
Less Non-current Liabilities			
Bank loan			(30,000)
NET ASSETS			193,887
EQUITY			
Issued Share Capital			
250,000 ordinary shares of 50p each fully paid			125,000
Capital Reserve			
Share premium			30,000
Revenue Reserve			
Retained earnings			38,887
TOTAL EQUITY			193,887

W1 Depreciation: £36,000 + £25,200

W2 Other payables: loan interest £900 owing + tax provision £5,854

7.

Note	Profit for the year	Retained earnings	Total equity	Current assets	Current liabilities
(a)	increase £3,000	increase £3,000	increase £3,000	increase £3,000	no change
(b)	decrease £100,000	decrease £100,000	decrease £100,000	no change	no change
(c)	increase £10,000	increase £10,000	increase £10,000	increase £10,000	no change
(d)	decrease £40,000	decrease £40,000	decrease £40,000	no change	increase £40,000

CHAPTER 18: FINANCIAL RATIOS

1. (a) *Formula*

$$\frac{\text{Cost of sales}}{\text{Average inventory}} \quad \text{or} \quad \frac{\text{Average inventory}}{\text{Cost of sales}} \times 365$$

Calculation

Average inventory = (10,350 + 14,150) ÷ 2 = 12,250

Rate of inventory turnover =

$$\frac{73,750}{12,250} = 6 \text{ times per year or } \frac{12,250}{73,750} \times 365 = 61 \text{ days}$$

(b)
- The rate of inventory turnover has fallen from 8 times per year to 6 times per year.
- This means that inventory is being sold more slowly this year.
- On the face of it, decreasing inventory turnover indicates a less efficient business as inventory is in the shop for longer before being sold.

2.

	Current ratio	Liquid capital ratio
Trade payables	✔	✔
Inventory	✔	
Tax liabilities	✔	✔
Other payables	✔	✔

answers - Chapter 18

3. (a) (i) *Formula*

   $$\frac{\text{Current assets}}{\text{Current liabilities}}$$

   Calculation

   $$\frac{105{,}630 + 162{,}940}{77{,}620 + 134{,}230} = \frac{268{,}570}{211{,}850} = 1.27:1$$

   (ii) *Formula*

   $$\frac{\text{Current assets} - \text{Inventory}}{\text{Current liabilities}}$$

   Calculation

   $$\frac{162{,}940}{77{,}620 + 134{,}230} = \frac{162{,}940}{211{,}850} = 0.77:1$$

   (b) <u>Current ratio</u>
   - Capper Ltd has £1.27 of current assets for each £1 of current liabilities.
   - This is lower than the industry average of £1.80 for each £1 of current liabilities.
   - Capper Ltd must investigate the make-up of its inventory, trade receivables, and trade payables as a low current ratio could make it difficult for the company to pay its trade payables in the future.

   <u>Liquid capital ratio</u>
   - Capper Ltd has 77p of liquid assets for each £1 of current liabilities.
   - This is lower than the industry average of 90p of liquid assets for each £1 of current liabilities.
   - Capper Ltd must investigate the make-up of its trade receivables and trade payables as a low liquid capital ratio could make it difficult for the company to pay its trade payables in the future.

   (c)
   - When goods are sold on credit there is a timing difference between making the sale/recording the profit and receiving payment for the sale. This timing difference – based on the accruals concept – has to be financed by the business.
   - When goods are bought on credit there is a timing difference between making the purchase and paying for the goods. This timing difference is a benefit to the business but it is usually less than the cost to the business of financing sales.
   - Prepaid expenses – based on the accruals concept – increase the profit for the year, but the expense has been paid for from the bank, so reducing the bank balance.
   - Capital expenditure on non-current assets reduces the bank balance by a greater amount than the depreciation charge for the asset shown in the income statement.
   - Repayment of loans reduces the bank balance but has little effect on profitability (although loan interest paid may be reduced).
   - Payment of dividends reduces the bank balance but has no effect on profit for the year.

4. (a)   *Formula*

$$\frac{\text{Gross profit}}{\text{Revenue}} \times 100$$

Calculation

$$\frac{72{,}000}{240{,}000} \times 100 = 30\%$$

(b)   *Formula*

$$\frac{\text{Profit for the year}}{\text{Revenue}} \times 100$$

Calculation

$$\frac{9{,}600}{240{,}000} = 100 = 4\%$$

(c)   *Formula*

$$\frac{\text{Average inventory} \times 365}{\text{Cost of sales}} \quad \text{or} \quad \frac{\text{Cost of sales}}{\text{Average inventory}}$$

Calculation

Average inventory = (22,000 + 26,000) ÷ 2 = 24,000

Rate of inventory turnover = $\frac{24{,}000}{168{,}000} \times 365 = 52$ days or $\frac{168{,}000}{24{,}000} = 7$ times per year

(d)   <u>Gross profit margin</u>
Possible actions to improve ratio:
- increase selling prices
- reduce buying prices
- a combination of both

Problems:
- increased selling prices may reduce sales and the profitability of the business
- reducing buying prices may mean that current suppliers will not continue to supply the product; also the quality of the product may be lowered

<u>Profit in relation to revenue</u>
Possible actions to improve ratio:

- increase gross profit margin
- reduce expenses
- a combination of both

Problems:
- may be difficult to reduce expenses such as wages
- reducing expenses may affect sales, eg a cut in advertising

Rate of inventory turnover

Possible actions to improve ratio:
- reduce inventory levels
- reduce buying prices
- a combination of both

Problems:
- reducing inventory levels could result in items being 'out-of-stock', which will impact on profitability
- reducing buying prices may mean a lower quality of product, which may impact on sales and profitability

5. (a) (i) *Formula*

$$\frac{\text{Trade receivables}}{\text{Credit sales}} \times 365 \text{ days}$$

Calculation

$$\frac{34{,}300}{357{,}700} \times 365 = 35 \text{ days}$$

(ii) *Formula*

$$\frac{\text{Trade payables}}{\text{Credit purchases}} \times 365 \text{ days}$$

Calculation

$$\frac{27{,}650}{258{,}775} \times 365 = 39 \text{ days}$$

(b) Trade receivable days
- Friel Ltd receives payment from trade receivables in 35 days on average.
- This is shorter than the industry average of 37 days.
- In general, the shorter the period the better, and this could indicate that Friel Ltd is more efficient at collecting debts than competitors, or that the company offers shorter terms than others within the industry. Either way, this could mean that Friel Ltd may be losing customers to their competitors.

Trade payable days
- Friel Ltd pays trade payables in 39 days on average.
- This is longer than the industry average of 33 days.
- Whilst longer trade payable days are advantageous to the bank balance, it may mean that Friel is not taking advantage of any cash discounts offered for quick settlement. Also, unless Friel Ltd has negotiated longer credit terms, it may be that suppliers will be reluctant to supply the company until outstanding amounts have been paid – this could be detrimental to Friel's sales and customer service.

Conclusion

As Friel's trade receivable days are shorter than the industry average and trade payable days are longer, there should be no adverse effect on the company's bank balance when compared with their competitors.

MANAGEMENT ACCOUNTING
ANSWERS

CHAPTER 19: BUDGETING AND BUDGETARY CONTROL

1.

Statements	Incremental budgeting	Zero-based budgeting
The budget 'starts from scratch'		✔
Inefficiencies and overspending are identified and avoided		✔
An increase is applied to last period's budget figures	✔	
The budget may include continuing activities that are uneconomic	✔	

2. **(a)** Budgets will provide benefits both for the business, and also for its managers and staff:
- budgets assist with planning
- budgets communicate and co-ordinate
- budgets help with decision-making
- budgets can be used to monitor and control
- budgets can be used to motivate

(b) Most businesses will benefit from the use of budgets, but there are a number of limitations to be aware of:
- the benefit of the budget must exceed its cost
- budget information may not be accurate
- budgets may demotivate
- budgets may lead to disfunctional management
- budgets may be set at too low a level

(c) Management can control the business through the use of variances. A variance is the budgeted cost, revenue or profit minus the actual cost, revenue or profit.

Management will be concerned with significant variances which are reported to the appropriate level of management within the business. This system of management by exception means that managers will act on variances that are significant, ie outside the tolerance limits, and investigative action will be taken.

3.

Statements	Favourable variance	Adverse variance
Budgeted revenue £35,000; actual revenue £34,000		✔
Actual costs £15,500; budgeted costs £16,000	✔	
Budgeted profit £46,000; actual profit £47,000	✔	
Budgeted costs £12,000; actual costs £11,500	✔	

4.

James Martland
Budgeted Income Statement for the year ending 31 December 20-4

	£	£
Revenue (W1) (228,000 units)		3,762,000
Less Cost of sales:		
Opening inventory (18,000 units)	126,000	
Add Purchases (W3) (227,100 units)	1,653,288	
Less Closing inventory (W2) (17,100 units)	124,488	
		1,654,800
Gross profit		2,107,200
Less Expenses:		
Wages (W4)	445,200	
General expenses (W5)	348,450	
Rent	225,000	
Depreciation (W6)	150,000	
Carriage outwards (W7)	205,200	
		1,373,850
Profit for the year		733,350

Workings: W1 (240,000 units x 0.95) x (£15 per unit x 1.1)

W2 (228,000 units x 18,000 units ÷ 240,000 units) x (£7 per unit x 1.04)

W3 (228,000 units + 17,100 – 18,000) x £7.28 (ie £7 per unit x 1.04)

W4 £420,000 x 1.06

W5 £345,000 x 1.01

W6 (£800,000 - £200,000) x 25%

W7 228,000 units x £0.90

5. (a)

Sylwia Sipkova
Budgeted Statement of Financial Position as at 31 December 20-6

	£	£
Non-current Assets		120,000
Less depreciation for year W1		24,000
Net book value		96,000
Current Assets		
Inventory W2	36,750	
Trade receivables W3	54,000	
Bank (see part (b))	29,500	
	120,250	
Less Current Liabilities		
Trade payables W4	49,000	
Net Current Assets		71,250
NET ASSETS		167,250
FINANCED BY		
Capital		
Opening capital		165,000
Add Profit for the year W5		37,250
Less Drawings		35,000
		167,250

Workings: W1 £30,000 ÷ £150,000 = 20% reducing balance depreciation; for 20-6 £120,000 x 20% = £24,000

W2 Purchases £294,000 ÷ 12 months x 1.5 months

W3 Revenue £432,000 ÷ 12 months x 1.5 months

W4 Purchases £294,000 ÷ 12 months x 2 months

W5 Revenue £432,000 − Cost of sales £287,250 (Opening inventory £30,000 + Purchases £294,000 − Closing inventory £36,750) − Expenses £107,500

(b)

	£	£
Opening bank balance (31 December 20-5)		10,000
Add receipts from trade receivables:		
opening trade receivables	65,000	
+ revenue	432,000	
– closing trade receivables	54,000	
		443,000
Less payments to trade payables:		
opening trade payables	60,000	
+ purchases	294,000	
– closing trade payables	49,000	
		(305,000)
Less expenses:		
income statement	107,500	
– depreciation for the year	24,000	
		(83,500)

> note that depreciation for the year is excluded because it is a non-cash expense

Less drawings taken by Sylwia Sipkova	(35,000)
Closing bank balance (31 December 20-6)	**29,500**

CHAPTER 20: MARGINAL COSTING AND BREAK-EVEN

1. A

2.

Term	Description
Profit or loss	Contribution minus fixed costs
Variable costs	Costs where the total cost varies in proportion with output
Break-even revenue	Break-even units x selling price per unit

3. B

4. (a) 400 units (£15 – £10 = £5 contribution per unit; £2,000 fixed costs ÷ £5)
   (b) £750 (550 units x £5 contribution = £2,750 – £2,000 fixed costs)

5. (a) £4.00 per unit, ie £100,000 ÷ 25,000 units
   (b) £1.60 per unit, ie (£100,000 – £60,000) ÷ 25,000 units
   (c) Sales revenue per unit – variable costs per unit
   (d) £2.40 per unit, ie £4.00 – £1.60
   (e) £24,000 forecast profit, ie (£2.40 x 35,000 units) – £60,000 fixed costs

6. (a)

The break-even point in units next month	20,000 units
The break-even point in sales revenue next month	£400,000
The estimated profit if 30,000 units are made and sold next month	£50,000

- break-even point in units next month

$$\frac{\text{fixed costs (£)}}{\text{contribution per unit (£)}} = \frac{£100,000}{£5} = 20,000 \text{ units}$$

- break-even point in sales revenue next month

  20,000 units x selling price £20 per unit = £400,000

- estimated profit if 30,000 units are made and sold next month

  30,000 units x £5 contribution = £150,000 - £100,000 fixed costs = £50,000

(b)

The budgeted output for next month	£25,000
The maximum output for next month	£75,000

Workings:

		Budgeted output (25,000 units)	Maximum output (35,000 units)
		£	£
	revenue (at £20 each)	500,000	700,000
minus	variable costs (at £15 each)	375,000	525,000
equals	contribution (to fixed costs and profit)	125,000	175,000
minus	monthly fixed costs	100,000	100,000
equals	profit for month	25,000	75,000

7. (a) 2,000 units (£28 – £16 = £12 contribution per unit; £24,000 ÷ £12)
   (b) £56,000 (2,000 units x £28)
   (c) £18,000 (3,500 units x £12 contribution = £42,000 – £24,000 fixed costs)
   (d) The break-even point will decrease

8.

Batches produced and sold	1,000	1,200	2,000
	£	£	£
Revenue	35,000	42,000	70,000
Variable costs:			
• Direct materials	7,500	9,000	15,000
• Direct labour	10,500	12,600	21,000
• Overheads	6,000	7,200	12,000
Semi-variable costs:			
• Variable element	1,500	1,800	3,000
• Fixed element	3,000	3,000	3,000
Total cost	28,500	33,600	54,000
Total profit	6,500	8,400	16,000

CHAPTER 21: DECISION-MAKING SITUATIONS

1. **A**

2. **A**

3. (a) *Total cost per seat (based on sixty seats sold)*

		£
direct materials	£15.00 x 60	900.00
direct labour	£10.00 x 60	600.00
fixed overheads		3,500.00
TOTAL COST		5,000.00

The total cost per seat is £5,000 ÷ 60 = £83.33

(b) *Marginal cost per seat*

	£
direct materials	15.00
direct labour	10.00
MARGINAL COST (per seat)	25.00

(c) *Profit or loss if no further tickets sold*

	£
revenue 60 seats at £100 each	6,000.00
less total cost (see above)	5,000.00
PROFIT	1,000.00

(d)

MERCIA AIRWAYS
income statement for flight MA 005

	60 seats sold £	60 seats + 30 sold to travel firm £	60 seats + 40 sold to newspaper £
Revenue for flight:			
60 seats at £100 each	6,000	6,000	6,000
30 seats at £45 each	–	1,350	–
40 units at £35 each	–	–	1,400
	6,000	7,350	7,400
Less Costs:			
Direct materials (£15 per passenger)	900	1,350	1,500
Direct labour (£10 per passenger)	600	900	1,000
Fixed overheads	3,500	3,500	3,500
PROFIT	1,000	1,600	1,400

Flight MA 005 to Rome

- Two proposals for the 40 unsold seats on next week's flight:
    - to sell approximately 30 seats at £45 each to the travel firm
    - to sell all 40 seats to the local newspaper at £35 each
- The income statement shows
    - if no further seats are sold the profit will be £1,000
    - if sold to the travel firm, the contribution (selling price – marginal cost) is 30 seats x (£45 – £25) = £600, which gives a profit figure of £1,600
    - if sold to the newspaper, the contribution is 40 seats x (£35 – £25) = £400, which gives a profit figure of £1,400

Conclusion

- The offer from the travel firm should be taken up, while the newspaper offer should not be considered on this occasion.
- With contributions of £20 per seat from the travel firm and £10 from the newspaper, provided that the flight firm can sell more than 20 seats, the contribution will be greater than that from the newspaper.

4. (a) *Total cost*

	£
direct materials (per pair)	20.00
direct labour (per pair)	18.00
fixed overheads (£200,000 ÷ 12,500 pairs)	16.00
TOTAL COST (per pair)	54.00

Marginal cost

	£
direct materials (per pair)	20.00
direct labour (per pair)	18.00
MARGINAL COST (per pair)	38.00

Profit or loss at existing production of 12,500 pairs of boots, see below.

(b)

THE LAST COMPANY LTD
Income statement

	Existing production 12,500 pairs of boots £	Existing production + 2,500 pairs @ £45 each £	Existing production + 5,000 pairs @ £37 each £
Revenue (per week):			
12,500 pairs at £60 each	750,000	750,000	750,000
2,500 pairs at £45 each	–	112,500	–
5,000 pairs at £37 each	–	–	185,000
	750,000	862,500	935,000
Less Production costs:			
Direct materials (£20 per pair)	250,000	300,000	350,000
Direct labour (£18 per pair)	225,000	270,000	315,000
Fixed overheads	200,000	200,000	200,000
PROFIT	75,000	92,500	70,000

Offer from Zambesi Limited

- Two contracts offered by Zambesi Limited for the 'Snowdon' range:
  - either 2,500 pairs at £45 per pair
  - or 5,000 pairs at £37 per pair
- The income statement for planned sales, together with the two offers shows:
  - if either offer is not taken up, profits next year are expected to be £75,000

- if 2,500 pairs are sold to Zambesi at £45 per pair, the contribution (selling price – marginal cost) is 2,500 x (£45 – £38) = £17,500; thus profits increase by £17,500 to £92,500

- if 5,000 pairs are sold to Zambesi at £37 per pair, the contribution is 5,000 (£37 – £38) = (£5,000); this price of £37 is below our marginal cost of £38; thus profits fall by £5,000 to £70,000

Conclusion

- The offer of 2,500 pairs at £45 per pair should be taken up, while the offer of 5,000 pairs at £37 should be rejected. This follows the principle that, once the fixed overheads have been recovered from normal sales, provided that additional units can be sold at a price above marginal cost, then profits will increase.

5. Financial implications

	£	£
Revenue 1,500 units x £220.00		330,000
Less variable costs:		
Material C: 1,500 x £66	99,000	
Material D: 1,500 x £15	22,500	
*Skilled labour: 2,450 hours at £30	73,500	
Semi-skilled labour 4,500 hours at £15	67,500	
		262,500
		67,500
Less shipping and insurance		14,500
Profit on order		53,000

* Skilled labour hours calculation:

1,500 x 2 hours	3,000 hours
Less unutilised hours	550 hours
	2,450 hours

- The order would produce an increase in the company's profit of (£53,000 ÷ £298,600 x 100) 17.75%. At the same time, it meets the objective of developing overseas sales and could be the entry into other overseas markets.

- For the order, the selling price is being discounted to £220.00 per unit when compared with a normal price of £275 per unit. Existing customers may learn of this and may well seek their own discounts.

- Potential future orders are larger, but much will depend on the price per unit.
- Are there any foreign exchange rate issues? If the order is priced and paid for in £s there is no problem.
- Future orders may not be paid in full upon shipping – in any case, credit control checks should be made on buyers. SecureWaste Limited may wish to take out export credit insurance for their overseas business.
- If large orders are received in future years, SecureWaste Limited must consider if it has the capacity to handle them. If not, consideration and the cost implications of adding more capacity should be made.
- There will be net current asset (working capital) considerations of this year's potential order and future orders. For example, increased inventory, trade payables, trade receivables, together with additional cash requirements to pay wages.

Non-financial implications

- Will skilled employees be prepared to work the necessary overtime hours at the rate suggested?
- The potential order this year has to be produced within four months and this will put pressure on employees and all aspects of the business.
- Will existing production and customer service suffer during the four-month period?
- Will quality of the product be maintained for both the overseas and current customers? What happens if the overseas customer is dissatisfied with quality?
- Is it possible to assess the likelihood of future orders materialising and at what selling price?
- If future orders materialise, the company needs to recruit and train new skilled labour. Is such labour available and what will be the training costs? More semi-skilled labour will also be required.
- Are material suppliers able to meet the requirements of increased orders? There is the potential to negotiate discounts with suppliers.
- Are there further overseas markets for SecureWaste Limited to consider?

Recommendation

- The order provides an opportunity to begin to develop overseas sales.
- On the figures given profit is expected to increase by £53,000.
- The existing under-utilisation of skilled labour will be taken up by the order.
- The order will require careful management of resources, particularly the timescale of four months and the overtime required from skilled employees.
- The company should take on this order but should evaluate progress before taking further orders.

answers - Chapter 21

6. A

7. (a) The total cost per set if 400 units are produced:

		£
Materials	5 kilos @ £20 per kilo x 375 sets	37,500
Labour	5 hours @ £15 per hour x 300 sets	22,500
	5 hours @ £25 per hour x 75 sets	9,375
PRIME COST		69,375
Fixed costs		26,250
TOTAL COST		95,625

Total cost per set £95,625 ÷ 375 sets = £255.00

(b) Original selling price:

	£
Materials per set	100.00
Labour per set	75.00
Fixed costs per set £26,250 ÷ 250 sets	105.00
TOTAL COST PER SET	280.00
Profit 60%	168.00
SELLING PRICE PER SET	448.00

New selling price:

	£
Total cost per set – see (a) above	255.00
Profit 60%	153.00
SELLING PRICE PER SET	408.00

Therefore the new selling price is £40 less than the original selling price.

8. (a)

Product	'People' £	'Animals' £	'Birds' £
Revenue per unit	60	27.50	17.50
minus: Variable costs per unit			
Direct materials	5	3	2
Direct labour	15	5	3.33
Variable overheads per unit	10	4.50	2.96
equals: Contribution per unit	30	15	9.21

(b) Break-even point for the 'People' range is:

$$\frac{\text{fixed costs (£)}}{\text{contribution per unit (£)}} = \frac{£45,400}{£30} = \underline{1,514 \text{ units}}$$

(c)

Product	'People'	'Animals'	'Birds'
Contribution per unit	£30	£15	£9.21
Labour hours per unit	1.5	0.5	0.333
Contribution per labour hour	£20	£30	£27.66

(d)
- Labour hours are the scarce resource here, with 2,800 hours available.
- To maximise profits, the company should maximise the contribution from each labour hour.
- The preferred order is 'Animals' (at £30 contribution per labour hour), 'Birds' (at £27.66), and 'People' (at £20).
- Optimum production plan:

Total hours available per month	2,800
less 'Animals', 2,000 units x 0.5 hours per unit	1,000
	1,800
less 'Birds', 2,700 units x 0.333 hours per unit	900
equals hours remaining to produce units of 'People'	900

Therefore production of 'People' at 1.5 hours per unit will be 600 units per month. This production plan does not allow for full production of the 'People' range.

9. (a)

	Newspapers and magazines £000	Books £000	Stationery £000	Total £000
Revenue	352	550	198	1,100
Less Variable costs:				
materials	155	246	122	523
labour	65	93	58	216
	220	339	180	739
Contribution	132	211	18	361
Less Fixed costs*	80	125	45	250
Profit/(Loss)	52	86	(27)	111
*apportioned to each section on the basis of revenue				

(b)
- On the basis of the information given, it would seem that the stationery section is making a loss.
- However, the stationery section makes a contribution of £18,000 to fixed costs and, if it was closed, it is likely that most of the fixed costs of the business will continue so reducing the overall profit of the business by £18,000 to £93,000 (a 16% decrease).
- Before a decision about closure of the stationery section is made, consideration should be made as to why its contribution is low when compared with the other two sections – could there be more efficient buying of inventory, or an increase in selling prices?
- If the section is to be closed a number of other factors come into play:
  - loss of goodwill from customers, as not all will continue to visit the shops (and sales of newspapers, magazines and books may be lost)
  - closure costs, including redundancy payments to staff not re-employed elsewhere in the other sections of the business
  - what to do with the space released by the stationery section – other products?

10. C

11. (a) Contribution sales (CS) ratio:

$$\frac{\text{contribution}}{\text{selling price}} = \frac{£75,000^*}{£250,000} = 0.3 \text{ or } 30\%$$

*revenue £250,000 – variable costs of £175,000

(b) Number of units to break-even:

$$\frac{\text{fixed costs}}{\text{CS ratio}} = \frac{£60,000}{0.3} = £200,000 \text{ revenue}$$

Each unit sells for £5.00, so the number of units to break-even is:

$$\frac{£200,000}{£5.00} = 40,000 \text{ units}^{**}$$

** revenue £200,000 – (variable costs at £3.50 per unit, £140,000 + fixed costs £60,000) = break-even

(c) Units and revenue to achieve profit of £45,000:

$$\frac{\text{fixed costs + target profit}}{\text{CS ratio}} = \frac{£60,000 + £45,000}{0.3} = \frac{70,000 \text{ units}}{\text{or £350,000 revenue}^{***}}$$

*** revenue £350,000 – (variable costs at £3.50 per unit, £245,000 + fixed costs £60,000) = £45,000 profit